Comments on other *Amazing Stories* from readers & reviewers

"You might call them the non-fiction response to Harlequin romances: easy to consume and potentially addictive."
Robert Martin, *The Chronicle Herald*

"Tightly written volumes filled with lots of wit and humour about famous and infamous Canadians."
Eric Shackleton, *The Globe and Mail*

"This is popular history as it should be...For this price, buy two and give one to a friend."
Terry Cook, a reader from Ottawa, on **Rebel Women**

"Stories are rich in description, and bristle with a clever, stylish realness."
Mark Weber, *Central Alberta Advisor,* on **Ghost Town Stories II**

"The resulting book is one readers will want to share with all the women in their lives."
Lynn Martel, *Rocky Mountain Outlook,* on *Women Explorers*

"[The books are] *long on plot and character and short on the sort of technical analysis that can be dreary for all but the most committed academic."*
Robert Martin, *The Chronicle Herald*

"A compelling read. Bertin ... has selected only the most intriguing tales, which she narrates with a wealth of detail."
Joyce Glasner, *New Brunswick Reader,* on **Strange Events**

"The heightened sense of drama and intrigue, combined with a good dose of human interest is what sets Amazing Stories *apart."*
Pamela Klaffke, *Calgary Herald*

AMAZING STORIES®

REBELS AGAINST TORIES IN UPPER CANADA 1837

By Maria da Silva
and Andrew Hind

James Lorimer & Company Ltd., Publishers
Toronto

James Lorimer & Company Ltd., Publishers acknowledge the support of the Ontario Arts Council. We acknowledge the financial support of the Government of Canada through the Canada Book Fund for our publishing activities. We acknowledge the support of the Canada Council for the Arts for our publishing program. We acknowledge the support of the Government of Ontario through the Ontario Media Development Corporation's Ontario Book Initiative.

Canada Council
for the Arts

Library and Archives Canada Cataloguing in Publication

da Silva, Maria
Rebels against Tories in Upper Canada 1837 / Maria da Silva and Andrew Hind.

(Amazing stories)
ISBN 978-1-55277-491-5

1. Canada—History—Rebellion, 1837-1838. I. Hind, Andrew
II. Title. III. Series: Amazing stories (Toronto, Ont.)

FC450.D36 2010   971.03'8   C2010-900771-9

James Lorimer & Company Ltd., Publishers
317 Adelaide Street West, Suite 1002
Toronto, Ontario
M5V 1P9
www.lorimer.ca

Printed and bound in Canada

Mixed Sources
Cert no. SW-COC-001271
© 1996 FSC

FSC

Contents

Prologue

A farmer pulled the collar of his coat up against the chill and pulled his hat down low over his face. Dusk was settling on the landscape and snowflakes began to swirl around the horns of his oxen. The farmer would rather be inside his cabin, warming himself by the fire and eating a hearty dinner, easing the pangs in his stomach and the numbness in his hands and feet. However, he knew he couldn't afford to lose the last fleeting moments of sunlight.

The farmer was late in planting and desperate to finish before the ground froze solid. The crops had failed this year and there was hardly enough to feed his family over the long winter that loomed ahead. He couldn't afford a second year of poor harvest, and he had little faith that the government would offer any assistance. After all, the politicians seemed more concerned with the interests of the rich landowners and businessmen in Toronto than with the welfare of poor farmers.

With a sigh, the farmer cracked the reins and urged the oxen into a lumbering walk. He was too intent on keeping the heavy plough steady to notice the young boy racing over the field toward him, waving a piece of paper. The excited cries of the boy finally caught his attention and he grabbed the paper from the panting youth. It was a proclamation dated

December 5 from the lieutenant-governor of the province, Sir Francis Bond Head. A rebellion led by William Lyon Mackenzie had broken out in the colony and Bond Head was calling upon the loyal militia of Upper Canada to come to his government's aid.

The farmer read the proclamation twice, his mind racing. He felt it was his duty, as a law-abiding citizen, to answer Bond Head's summons. But at the same time, what had the government ever done for him and his hungry family? What if William Lyon Mackenzie could deliver on his promise for a more equal Upper Canada, one where the rights and interests of common farmers and craftsmen were acknowledged?

It was a potentially life-altering decision, one which faced all men and women in Upper Canada in the early winter of 1837.

Introduction

The year 1837 was a troubled one in Upper Canada (as the province of Ontario was then known). There was political chaos, an economic crisis that caused widespread discontent, and rabble-rousing by firebrands intent on overturning the established government through revolution. Into this volatile mix came a new Lieutenant-Governor, Sir Francis Bond Head, whose abrasive style and lack of subtlety exacerbated the problem. Rebellion was now inevitable and, encouraged by William Lyon Mackenzie, violence finally erupted in December.

While the rebellion was brief and relatively bloodless, the repercussions of the sudden violence tore through Upper Canada, turning lives upside down, throwing peaceful communities into panic, and setting friends, neighbours and even family members against one another. In the process, it shaped Canadian history and the very nature of society.

Most accounts dealing with the Upper Canada Rebellion of 1837 focus on the colourful and controversial personality of William Lyon Mackenzie, the march of his ill-fated army down Yonge Street, and the crushing defeat at the Battle of Montgomery's Tavern a few short days later. Lost amongst all this are the individual stories of those whose lives were thrown into turmoil as a result of the uprising. Some individuals lost everything, some emerged as heroes or villains, and almost everyone—whether they actively took up arms or not—was touched by the enormity of the events.

Rebels Against Tories in Upper Canada 1837 addresses this common oversight by focusing on a number of individuals who were swept up by the tidal wave of events. Rather than important political figures, these are "common" people from a broad spectrum of society—retired army officers, women and children, farmers and craftsmen, Ojibwa natives, and tavernkeepers. Their experiences are dramatic and fraught with the tension of the times, sometimes heartbreaking, occasionally full of heart-pumping excitement, always enlightening of the impact the rebellion had on everyday lives.

In the following pages we meet some of these people and share their stories, study the still-debated causes and outcomes of the conflict, and follow the road that led Ontario on the path to violent uprising.

Chapter 1:
Causes of the Rebellion

There are countless reasons why hundreds of farmers and craftsmen decided to take up arms and oppose the lawful government of Upper Canada; each man had his own motivation, his own unique set of circumstances and beliefs. Nevertheless, we can trace the origins of the rebellion to a handful of societal ailments that, over a matter of years or even decades, slowly festered until by 1837 it had developed into a feverish anger that could not be suppressed.

Alone, any one of these issues would be divisive. Together, they conspired to pull Upper Canada apart, pitting neighbour against neighbour in a war of words and ideals that eventually evolved into a true war—one where losses weren't measured in political power or votes, but in human lives.

Government in the British Colonies

The roots of the rebellion of 1837 can be traced to the Constitutional Act of 1791, which saw the creation of both an elected body (the Legislative Assembly) and an appointed body (the Legislative Council) within Upper Canada. While the elected assembly had limited powers, there was much overlap between its duties and that of the Legislative Council, and they were jointly responsible for passing legislation. This naturally created a climate in which strong conflict was almost inevitable, especially since elected bodies have a tendency to regard their views as paramount; they, in theory at least, represent the will of the people.

Complicating the situation was the manner in which elections were held. Voting was held in public places (often in a tavern), so it was extremely easy to influence voters by way of threats or bribes. Naturally, it was the wealthiest and most powerful members of society, those who had the money and influence to sway votes, who reaped the greatest benefit from the practice of public ballot-casting. In fact, one of the sparks that set off the flames of rebellion was the election of 1836, which was widely held to have been grossly corrupt in favour of the Tories.

Adding to the political chaos was the presence of a

lieutenant-governor, appointed by the Colonial Office in England, in whom ultimate power in the colony was vested. One of his greatest responsibilities was the appointment of government ministers in Upper Canada (the Executive Council), but he usually selected wealthy and influential members of prominent colonial families without consultation with the ordinary people or their elected representatives.

When the lieutenant-governor was a man of political acumen, with strong leadership qualities but also a willingness to listen and compromise, the government could function smoothly. However, this was not often the case, and because lieutenant-governors were drawn from the ruling classes themselves they tended to align themselves with the interests of the Family Compact.

Privileges of the Family Compact

Living in their comfortable mansions in Toronto, members of the Family Compact—who represented only a tiny fraction of the population of Upper Canada—dominated the Executive Council and the Legislative Council (neither of which was elected), the judiciary, the senior civil service, and even much of the House of Assembly. The members of this oligarchy had the ear of successive governors and used that influence to increase their stranglehold on colonial affairs. They dispensed favours to their friends, directed British policy to their own advantage, controlled the best land, and built vital infrastructure—such as roads and canals—in the interests of businessmen rather than farmers.

It was only natural that the masses, particularly farmers and craftsmen living beyond the borders of the provincial capital, should grow resentful of these privileged individuals and demand a more equitable share in the political and economic arena. They noticed that much of Upper Canada remained a frontier backwater, slow in developing and poorly managed; as the years passed and little progress was made in extending civilization beyond the borders of Toronto, despondency set in.

Members of the Family Compact surely saw the growing sense of disenfranchisement among the general public, but they saw real danger in reform and adamantly refused any move to grant more power to the people. They believed that if the poorly educated, uncultured masses had power, the result would be chaos. They saw in the American Revolution the violence that ensued when democracy reared its head. They were ultra-conservative in ways of politics and the economy, and their views were at odds with those of the vast majority.

American Influence and Republicanism

Since the 1790s, revolutionary fervor had swept Europe and it was inevitable that lofty ideals concerning democracy and individual rights would come across to Canada with the masses of immigrants that flowed into the British colony. Similar ideas came north from the United States, carried to Upper Canada by the thousands of American settlers who came to the province in the last decade of the eighteenth century and the first of the nineteenth. While the vast majority of American settlers were sincere in their pledges of loyalty to their adopted country, there is no doubt that deep-rooted American independence and republicanism prevented complete acquiescence to British political institutions.

Both before and after the War of 1812, the government of Upper Canada continued to fear what it suspected might be a growing interest in American-inspired republicanism in the province. After an initial group of about seven thousand United Empire Loyalists were thinly settled across the province in the mid-1780s, a far larger number of American settlers came in the 1790s when Lieutenant-Governor John Graves Simcoe offered cheap land grants to promote settlement. Although these settlers, known as "late Loyalists," were required to take an oath of allegiance to the Crown in order to obtain land, their fundamental political allegiances were always considered dubious. By 1812 this had become acutely problematic since the American settlers outnumbered the original Loyalists by more than ten to one. Following the war, the provincial government took active steps to prevent Americans from swearing allegiance, thereby making them ineligible to obtain land grants. In the years after the war relations between the elected Legislative Assembly, which included a great many American-born or American-descended individuals, and the appointed Legislative Council became increasingly strained over issues of both immigration and taxation.

The increasingly republican tone of William Lyon Mackenzie's speeches, especially after 1836, only heightened the establishment's fears over his intentions and those of his fellow reformers. This deeply ingrained suspicion made it difficult, if not impossible, to reach a political settlement that would have averted rebellion.

Allocation of Land

One of the most controversial issues in Upper Canada during the early nineteenth century was the allocation of land. A large percentage of land, and often the most appealing acreage, had been set aside either as "Crown Reserves" or for the support of the Anglican Church. These vast reserves of unworked land lowered the value of neighbouring farms because isolated farms were less efficient than farms close together. Also, people of other religious sects (particularly Methodists, Presbyterians and Roman Catholics) resented the preferential treatment of the Anglican Church.

At the same time, new settlers resented being allotted land in distant wilderness regions, isolated by poor roads and far from any semblance of civilization, when huge tracts

William Lyon Mackenzie

of potentially prosperous "Crown Reserves" remained idle. It must have been disheartening to pass by hundreds of acres of fallow fields, temptingly close to York and other towns, and then still have to make one's way a day or more into the interior, along progressively poorer roads and deep into the dark forests of the wilderness. This tree-shrouded land would determine success or failure in the New World. One can easily see why there was a growing tide of discontent against the inequitable nature of land allocation, which only grew stronger with each passing year as new settlers were pushed further and further into the untamed interior.

A Series of Unfortunate Events

The sense of hopelessness that gripped much of Upper Canada's populace was only aggravated by a cascade of unfortunate events during the 1830s. Cholera epidemics ravaged the province in 1832 and 1834, killing hundreds, and these were followed by several years of poor harvest owing to inhospitable weather. At the same time, farmers across the colony lost their main market for wheat, the sole export crop upon which they could reliably depend, when Britain began experiencing increased production at home and therefore needed to import far less grain from overseas. The resulting economic stagnation and hardship was most keenly felt by the small landholding farmers, and led to increased frustration with the lack of attention to their needs on the part of the colonial government.

In light of the situation in Upper Canada in 1837, it's actually a wonder that most people remained loyal to the regime that seemed to be doing so little on their behalf.

Chapter 2:
The Road to Rebellion

Rising Tensions: the 1830s

While the Reform movement had begun years earlier, during the 1830s it became increasingly clear that the interests of the governed were growing apart from those who were governing. As the gap widened the pace of events quickened, leading inexorably toward a crisis. The Tories (or conservatives) won a majority in the Assembly in the 1831 elections, leaving Reformers despairing of any hope of making changes. Frustrated, William Lyon Mackenzie, the red-headed newspaperman and politician around whom the Reform movement coalesced, made a trip to England in the summer of 1832 to present his grievances to the Colonial Office. He returned to Upper Canada without getting any real satisfaction for his efforts, but found some comfort in knowing that at least now the Colonial Office was aware that all was not well in Upper Canada.

The Reformers won a majority in the Assembly in the October elections of 1834. At the same time, York was newly incorporated as the city of Toronto, which meant it would elect a municipal council. Mackenzie won the seat of mayor and, because of the Reformer majority in the Assembly, was able to resume his seat in the legislature from which he had been expelled due to his revolutionary leanings. All was looking well for the Reformer movement.

It was just a cruel illusion, however. Mackenzie's reputation for radicalism and firebrand antics were putting off moderates among his followers and cost him the position of mayor after only a single year. His speeches, in which he claimed that the government and Family Compact were committing "acts of tyranny and oppression," only incensed his opponents and made them more convinced that he was dangerous. Ironically, Mackenzie himself was becoming a liability to the peaceful, political resolution to the growing crisis that most Reformers craved.

In January 1836, Sir John Colborne was replaced as Lieutenant-Governor of Upper Canada by Sir Francis Bond Head. He arrived with a reputation as a reformer but quickly proved he wasn't. Bond Head allied himself with the Family Compact and developed a hatred for Mackenzie that was returned in kind. A military man, he expected people to follow orders and resented infringements upon his power. As a result, when the Reform Assembly stubbornly refused to approve his budget of 1836 until he addressed some of their complaints, Bond Head disbanded parliament on April 20. He further added to the crisis by staging a Tory triumph at the poll in August of that year, using blatant bribery and ballot-rigging to win.

By this point, Upper Canada was seething with tension. Among the rural craftsmen and farmers frustration and bitterness led to more open talk of rebellion. Their discontent simmered under the sweltering heat of the summer of 1837 and the fiery rants of Mackenzie and his followers. It was obvious that unless something was done soon the anger would boil over into armed revolt. Unfortunately, even while Mackenzie was drawing up a "Declaration of Independence of Upper Canada" and plotting an armed revolt, Bond Head refused to take his opponents seriously and did nothing to calm the situation.

Mackenzie's plans for open revolt were encouraged by a similar revolt that had broken out in Lower Canada (Quebec) under Louis-Jean Papineau, which seemed to be enjoying some success in battle. By sending all available regular army units in Upper Canada to Lower Canada to suppress the francophone uprising, Bond Head only emboldened the Reformers.

Many historians have been critical of Bond Head's decision, but there may have been some merit to his actions. There can be no doubt that the danger of revolt in Lower Canada, where there were few loyalist militia to draw upon, was far greater than of any potential uprising. In addition, he may well have feared that to set regular soldiers, coldly trained for war, against an assortment of rioting civilians could have resulted in gory repression with long-lingering after-effects. At least militia, who would be fighting against neighbours and even friends, would show some restraint.

Whatever his rationale, Bond Head's decision convinced Mackenzie that the time for rebellion had come and a date was fixed: December 7, 1837. As it happened, however, miscommunication caused rebels to begin assembling in Holland Landing on December 3, while Mackenzie was still rounding up support in distant townships. He was furious and wanted to countermand the order, but it was too late—rebels under Samuel Lount were on the march and the rebellion was under way.

Outbreak of Rebellion and the Battle of Montgomery's Tavern

By December 4, only a few hundred men had answered Mackenzie's call to assemble at Montgomery's Tavern. They were tired from the long march, hungry, and poorly organized. Many were disgusted by the lack of preparation: there were no arms, no supplies, and none of the promised food awaiting. Because of the premature launch of the rebellion the man appointed to command the rebel army, Anthony van Egmond, hadn't yet arrived.

Worse, neither Mackenzie nor his second-in-command, Samuel Lount, could agree on exactly when they should march on Toronto. Impatient, Mackenzie pushed for an immediate attack, while Lount suggested they wait for more men to filter in to bolster their numbers. In the end, they decided to sleep on it. Their indecisiveness gave away the vital element of surprise and cost them their only real opportunity to seize Toronto before the loyalist forces could assemble in its defence.

When Mackenzie awoke on the fifth, he found that overnight his motley army had swelled to more than five hundred rebels, and he determined it was large enough to capture the city. And yet, inexplicably, he still dawdled. It wasn't until shortly after noon that the rebel army advanced down Yonge Street toward City Hall and the rich store of arms and ammunition held there. At Gallows Hill (Yonge and St. Clair) they were met by representatives of Bond Head bearing a flag of truce. It was a tense exchange of words. Mackenzie explained the rebels' demands, while the government officials responded by offering amnesty for those rebels who turned themselves in and the severest of punishment for those who refused. Neither side was willing to negotiate, so

Rebel re-enacters skirmishing along the road to Toronto.

the parley was brief and pointless. An armed confrontation was now inevitable.

As soon as the parley had ended, the rebels advanced once again, soon reaching the tollgate at Yonge and Bloor. There Mackenzie, in a fit of spite, burned the house of noted loyalist Dr. Horne, for no reason but his association with the Bank of Upper Canada. He would have put Sheriff Jarvis's home, Rosedale, to the torch as well had Lount not prevented it.

Mackenzie was once again gripped with indecisiveness. Instead of continuing the advance on Toronto, for some reason he elected to turn the rebel army around and trek several miles north again to make camp. With each hour he dawdled, the loyalist position grew stronger and his own weakened. During the afternoon of the fifth, for example, a steamer from Hamilton arrived bearing sixty-five well-armed and well-drilled militia under the able command of Allan MacNab, while other contingents were expected to filter in over the next few days.

Perhaps realizing they were frittering away any chance of success, at six in the evening and with darkness gathering around them, Samuel Lount led several hundred men toward Toronto. As they marched down the hill at Mount Pleasant, the rebels "saw a wagonload of cordwood standing on the opposite rise, and supposing it to be a piece of artillery loaded to the muzzle with grape or canister, these brave warriors leaped the fences right and left like squirrels, and could by no effort of their officers be induced again to advance."

It was only with extreme effort that Lount was able to urge his men out from behind the trees where they cowered and back into formation. Jittery and on edge, the rebels cautiously probed their way further down Yonge as far as Maitland Street. Here, first contact with loyalist forces was made, this time for real.

Sheriff Jarvis had gathered a party of twenty-seven loyalist volunteers and hidden them alongside the road in the garden of William Sharp. It was a pitifully small band with which to confront the rebel army, but Jarvis gambled that in the darkness it would have been impossible for the enemy to know just how greatly they outnumbered his own forces. The volunteers lay in ambush until the rebels were close, and then opened up with a volley of musketry. Muzzle flashes lit up the darkness. The roar of musketry rolled across the landscape. Wounded men cried in agony and others yelled in surprise or anger. Chaos reigned.

The rebel riflemen in the front ranks returned fire in good order, then fell flat to allow the second rank to fire over them. This gesture, a standard military maneuver, was misinterpreted in the dark by the bulk of the untrained rebels, who thought gunfire had devastated the entire front row and with it their leaders. The rebels panicked and fled, carrying two wounded with them (both of whom subsequently died) and leaving Sharon native James Henderson lying face-first in the mud, dead.

Mackenzie was sickened by the ineptitude of his men. In his account of the action, he wrote: "... many of the country people, ... when they saw the riflemen in front falling down and heard the firing, they imagined that those who fell were the killed and wounded by the enemy's fire, and took to their heels ... This was almost too much for the human patience. The city would have been ours in an hour, probably without firing a shot ... But 800 ran ... and unfortunately ran the wrong way."

Though only a few men had been killed and wounded in

the brief skirmish, the main casualty was morale. In the face of unexpected resistance and a demoralizing defeat, several hundred deserted. Wednesday, December 6, was another day of indecision and disorganization as the remainder of the shaken rebel forces fell back to regroup and lick their wounds at Montgomery's Tavern. Mackenzie fared little better than his men, and was clearly becoming dispirited and unglued. "Little Mac conducted himself like a crazy man all the time we were at Montgomery's," a rebel later recounted. "He went about storming and screaming like a lunatic, and many of us felt certain he was not right in his senses."

A brief surge in morale occurred on the morning of the seventh when Colonel Anthony Van Egmond arrived from Goderich to take command of the rebel army. Unlike Mackenzie and Lount, he was an old campaigner with more than a decade of experience during the Napoleonic Wars and had a sound grasp of military tactics. The men knew his reputation and felt at last they had a capable leader, one perhaps who could salvage victory from a rebellion that had been ill-planned and poorly handled from the start.

Van Egmond's position was becoming desperate, however. Apart from dwindling supplies and lack of arms, the number of rebels dwindled with desertions, whereas Bond Head's forces were increasing almost daily. By the seventh his forces numbered 1,500, and continued to grow as volunteers arrived in town almost on an hourly basis.

There seemed every reason for Van Egmond to retreat, for the odds were heavily stacked against him, and indeed that is what Bond Head expected him to do. But for various reasons—some of them good ones—Van Egmond was not prepared to fall back. Instead, he elected to meet the enemy half a mile south of Montgomery's Tavern and bet the rebellion on a single, desperate roll of the dice.

Colonel Van Egmond prepared for the inevitable clash as best he could, knowing full well that an army that outnumbered his own by almost three to one was already advancing on him. He posted 150 of his precious musket-armed men in the woods on the west side of Yonge, while another sixty men with firearms lined up behind a split-rail fence at the Paul Fry Inn on the east side. The majority of Mackenzie's rebels, numbering three hundred, were placed further back in the shelter of Montgomery's Tavern itself. Armed with nothing more than hand weapons, they could play no decisive role in the coming battle.

At noon, the loyalist force, led by Colonel Fitzgibbon, marched into sight and began to form for battle. Fitzgibbon had two artillery pieces under his command, and immediately had them unlimbered and brought forward for action. The first shot beheaded rebel Ludovic Wideman of Stouffersville (Stouffville), while the second went through the roof of the Paul Fry Inn. With this display of lethality, rebel courage began to falter. It was apparent that they would be cut to pieces if they remained in their positions.

Fitzgibbon sensed that his opponents were shaken and gave the order to advance his infantry. The midday sun reflected off hundreds of bayonets as government troops strode forward. The rebels in the woods and behind the fence admired this display of military prowess for a few moments, then abandoned their positions and retreated in disarray toward the tavern. The sight of the advance guard in flight caused the poorly-armed rebels at the tavern to panic and flee in all directions through the woods.

Within twenty minutes, the rebel army was defeated, its men scattered to the breeze, and the rebellion crushed. twelve insurgents were killed and another twenty-four wounded; there were no casualties among the government troops. In an act of spite, Bond Head ordered his men to torch Montgomery's Tavern and the home of David Gibson, one of Mackenzie's most vocal supporters.

Aftermath

The rebellion was essentially crushed at Montgomery's Tavern, but the crisis was not yet over. Despite a £1,000 reward for his capture, William Lyon Mackenzie evaded his pursuers and escaped to the United States. Assisted by American sympathizers who offered funding, armaments, and political support, he organized his few remaining followers on Navy Island in the Niagara River and from there issued a proclamation that promised three hundred acres of land and $100 in silver to anyone who volunteered for the cause. He clearly was not yet ready to give up the fight.

Upper Canada remained extremely tense into 1838, as militia officers sent detachments to track down rebel threats that were not much more than shadows. On the merest suspicion presumed traitors were jailed, languishing there for months without trial. There was very real fear of further unrest, but in the end these fears proved groundless. The majority of Upper Canadians remained loyal to their provincial government and demonstrated that, whatever feelings might remain for Reform objectives, few wanted to achieve them by armed violence.

To the surprise of many, there was no Tory reign of terror against rebels and their sympathizers. True, hundreds were rounded up and imprisoned, and some were exiled to Van Diemen's Land (Tasmania), but only two men— Samuel Lount and Peter Matthews—faced the traditional punishment for treason: the hangman's noose. In time, there was even a full pardon granted to everyone else involved, Mackenzie included. It was an incredibly lenient response to rebellion, an indication that the government realized the reformers had some legitimate complaints.

At this point, events became international in nature. American sympathizers established so-called Hunter Lodges to form an army intended to invade Canada and spread

American republicanism. Raids were carried out into Upper and Lower Canada over the next two years. Canadian loyalists in turn made a raid across the Niagara River to capture and burn a rebel supply ship, the *Caroline*. These border incidents raised tensions between Britain and the United States, almost leading to war.

By 1840, calm had descended upon Upper Canada. Raiding from the United States had all but ceased, the rebels of 1837 had been pardoned, economic depression had given way to prosperity and a new wave of British immigration, and changes were made in the political system that made it somewhat more democratic (though it would take many more years to achieve full responsible government). The short-lived rebellion was little more than a bad memory that people desperately tried to put behind them; in the end, they did it so well that Mackenzie's Rebellion was all but forgotten.

Chapter 3:
Colonels Moodie and Bridgford

Despite rising tensions and worrisome signs throughout the summer that matters were at breaking point, Lieutenant Governor Sir Francis Bond Head refused to believe that rebellion was about to break out in 1837. He dismissed such notions with a wave of the hand, and made no attempt to prepare for what certainly seemed to most onlookers as an inevitable outbreak of violence. He could have called out elements of the loyalist militia, posted sentries to keep watch on roads leading into Toronto, or posted guards on key government buildings. That he did none of these things ensured that the rebellion, when it finally erupted, caught him and his advisors off guard. Mackenzie and his followers had achieved complete surprise.

In fact, the rebellion might well have succeeded if not for the heroic actions of Colonels Moodie and Bridgford who, upon learning of the advancing rebel army, risked their lives in a desperate nighttime ride to warn the government of the looming danger. That Bond Head had time to hastily gather enough forces to defend Toronto is owed largely to their actions that cold, dark December evening.

Colonel Moodie Rides into Legend

On Monday, December 4, 1837, Captain Hugh Stewart watched in amazement from the door of Crew's Tavern, just north of Richmond Hill, as dozens of armed men marched past. Some were armed with muskets, but most carried only spears or farming implements and all appeared weary and cold. This was the vanguard of Mackenzie's rebel force that had assembled near Holland Landing and was now heading south to Toronto. Stewart, a retired British naval officer, hurriedly sent runners out to area loyalists, summoning them to gather at the home of fifty-nine-year-old retired Colonel Robert Moodie.

Stewart arrived at Moodie's door out of breath and in a near panic. He quickly relayed to his friend the troubling news that the long-rumoured rebellion had finally erupted. No sooner had he finished than a mob of rebels, numbering around 125 individuals, gathered outside Moodie's home. The mob hurled insults toward the retired officers, threatening to kill them both and then ransack Moodie's home and burn it to the ground.

Colonel Moodie was not intimidated. He had faced death on several battlefields and would not be threatened by a mob of unruly civilians. Moodie calmly loaded a pair of pistols and put on the uniform he had last worn twenty-five years previously. Though the bright red jacket was tighter around the waist than it had once been, it still fit and somehow made him feel like the brave, dutiful officer of his youth. Wearing the uniform once again, with weapons tightly gripped in hand, caused decades-old memories of wartime experiences to suddenly resurface in the old soldier—memories of sacrifice, of fallen friends and comrades left on forgotten battlefields, of the responsibility of leadership. As the echoes of old battles washed over him, Moodie set his jaw, walked to the front door, and warned the rebels outside that the first man to enter his property would be shot on the spot.

The rebels had clearly not expected such courage, and their determination wavered. A tense standoff followed. Then, late in the afternoon, the mob resumed its march south. As soon as the rebel army was out of sight, village loyalists hastily met in Moodie's parlour to determine what action to take. It was unanimously decided that Lieutenant-Governor Sir Francis Bond Head must be made aware of the crisis, and tavern-keeper William Crew volunteered to be the one to go. He mounted a horse and raced off toward Toronto.

Around 6 p.m., however, word returned to Richmond Hill that Crew had been captured by some of Mackenzie's men at a barricade they had thrown across Yonge at what is today Eglinton Avenue. Matters were now desperate; the rebel army was dangerously close to the city and still the government was unaware of the threat. Colonel Moodie was aghast at the audacity of the rebels, and despite his advanced age decided to undertake an effort to warn the authorities. "I cannot think of the Governor and people of Toronto being murdered in their beds," he said bravely. "I'll do all I can to pass the rebels on the roads and save them."[1]

Frances Moodie, the Colonel's wife, who had been listening at the door, burst into the room at this point. She was on the verge of tears, begging her husband not to go. As a former officer, he may have a responsibility to his country, she argued, but he also had a responsibility to her and their family. His first priority was to remain at home and protect her from harm. Dutiful feelings of loyalty to British interests were swept aside by concerns for her aging husband. He had done his bit for King and Country, she pointed out between sobs. Leave the soldiering to younger men.

But Colonel Moodie wouldn't be dissuaded, even by the tears of his beloved wife. He couldn't neglect his responsibility. For him, the call of duty was impossible to ignore.

Soldiering was his business. It meant a sense of purpose and direction, power and authority, perhaps even a little excitement. He dearly loved his wife, but the opportunity to defend the interests of Great Britain once again was irresistible.

To calm Frances' fears, David Bridgford, another veteran of the war of 1812 and a close friend, and Captain Stewart volunteered to accompany Moodie. And so, as night settled upon the landscape, the three men saddled their horses, said goodbye to their wives, and without looking back raced off into the darkness and the unknown.

Robert Moodie's life had been defined by service to the Crown, and he saw this as just another duty he was required by honour to perform. Born in 1778 in Fifeshire, Scotland, he spent more than three decades in the British army.[2] He received a commission as an officer during the early years of the Napoleonic Wars, but was not destined to see any action in Europe. Instead, he was posted to Canada, where he helped to form the New Brunswick Fencibles.[3] Established in August, 1803, the regiment consisted of volunteers from New Brunswick, Nova Scotia, and Lower Canada (Quebec), and was intended for service in North America.

The New Brunswick Fencibles, and with them Colonel Robert Moodie, rose to prominence during the War of 1812. In the first year of the conflict the defences of Upper Canada (Ontario) barely held against the American invasion. To reinforce the troops there, it was decided to force-march six companies of the New Brunswick Fencibles (then known as the 104th Regiment) from Fredericton to Kingston in the middle of winter, a distance of hundreds of miles in the foulest of weather. Moodie accompanied the regiment during this extraordinary test of endurance, facing the blinding snowstorms and bone-aching cold alongside his men. He experienced their hunger-pangs, their fear of freezing to death while sleeping, their misery from never being dry, and their utter exhaustion from trudging day after day through knee-deep snow. As a result Moodie earned their trust and respect. He then took temporary command of the unit from May to December, leading them with distinction in the battles of Sackett's Harbour (May 29) and Beaver Dams (June 24).

When the 104th Regiment was disbanded in 1817 as part of peacetime cost-cutting measures, Colonel Moodie returned to England. After his military career came to an end in the early 1830s, he returned to Canada in 1835 and settled on Yonge Street in Richmond Hill. This small village was an ideal home for the patriotic veteran. The inhabitants were largely pro-British, staunchly loyal to the Crown and military-oriented. Moodie's home was distinctive with its huge flagpole from which flew an equally grand Union Jack, readily identifying it as the rallying point for area loyalists.

Colonel Moodie was greatly respected by his neighbours and well-liked, always ready with a thrilling anecdote about his military experiences in the War of 1812. He settled into a comfortable existence, undoubtedly missing the thrill of soldiering but finding satisfaction in more peaceful pursuits.

Unfortunately, the tranquility of retirement didn't grace Moodie for long. Two years after coming to Canada, in the midst of a cold December, he found himself once again in the service of the Crown during a time of war, racing desperately through a bitter evening to warn officials of an impending attack.

After departing from Richmond Hill, the three loyalists rode quickly through the night. Along the way, four other concerned citizens joined them. It was late in the evening when the small party reached Montgomery's Tavern, a well-known landmark on the road to Toronto. The men quickly pulled up on their reins, their horses skidding to a halt. There were dozens of campfires in the fields surrounding the tavern, and in their eerie glow hundreds of armed men could be seen. Moodie and his companions had stumbled upon the main rebel camp.

The loyalists debated their next course of action. They could go around the camp, which might take hours, or they could take the more direct route and race directly through the enemy ranks. Bridgford argued for the safer but longer route, while Moodie stressed that time was of the essence. In the end, the party split up. Bridgford and several companions veered off through the woods in order to circle the enemy force, while Moodie and Stewart kicked their mounts into action and rode hell-bent through the camp.

At the sight of the two charging horses, some of the rebels jumped to their feet and abandoned the warmth of their fires to race out onto the road into their path. They were determined to stop the riders from passing. Some were trampled by the sweaty, frenzied horses, but there were simply too many to barrel through. The swarming rebels grabbed hold of the horses' reins and ordered Moodie and Stewart to surrender.

"Who are you that dare stop me upon the Queen's highway?" challenged Moodie.[4]

"You'll find out that by and by," came a harsh reply. Moodie fired a pistol into the mob, and three shots quickly fired back.

"I'm shot, I'm a dead man," Moodie gasped, mortally wounded with two bullets lodged in his left side. He slid from his saddle and fell to the ground. He, along with Stewart, was taken prisoner and brought into Montgomery's Tavern. The rebels separated the two, holding them in separate rooms. Stewart begged for a doctor to be summoned to care for his friend, but John Montgomery, the hotel-keeper, refused. Enraged, Stewart asked to be allowed to tend to Moodie himself. He was only granted a brief visit.

"I found him lying on the floor in a small room, bleeding and writhing in agony," Stewart later wrote.[5] Colonel Moodie

Colonel Moodie's death outside Montgomery's Tavern.

suffered in pain for three hours, cold and alone, feverish, teeth gritted against the agony. He eventually succumbed to his injuries, but before he closed his eyes he had one final thought, that of his wife's loving arms holding him. It's said his final moments were peaceful, as if the pain miraculously lifted as his life slipped away. Colonel Robert Moodie was the rebellion's first casualty.

The heart-wrenching sounds of his agonizingly slow death, the cries for help and the moans of suffering had an unnerving effect upon those rebels gathering at the tavern. For many, Moodie's death was the first indication of the seriousness of the course of action they were committed to. No mere demonstration, this was war and in war people died, often painfully and brutally. Many of Mackenzie's men began to wonder whether, in the next few days, it might be them shrieking in agony as they stared death in the eye. The effect on morale was devastating.

Three days after his death a funeral for the fallen hero was held at Holy Trinity Church in Thornhill. The atmosphere in the region was so tense that, despite the protests of the presiding priest, all the bereaved carried swords, rifles, pistols, or farming implements in case rebels decided to disrupt the solemn ceremony. Over the years, Colonel Moodie's ill-fated ride down Yonge Street became a part of Canadian folklore, taking on a Paul Revere-type mystique. As a result, a century after his passing, a plaque was erected memorializing this brave and able military officer who had served many years in the defence of Canada and died doing so one last time; it's located on the east side of Yonge Street opposite Levendale Road in Richmond Hill.

Colonel David Bridgford Raises the Alarm

Since leaving Yonge Street, Colonel Bridgford and his companions had groped their way through dark shrouded woods and quickly skirted farm fields. Though the going was slow, they had yet to be detected by rebel patrols and Bridgford couldn't help but conclude that his decision to ride around behind the tavern, rather than force their way past the guards as Moodie had advocated, was the more prudent choice.

Suddenly, the sound of four gunshots pierced the night. Colonel Bridgford pulled up his horse. The gunfire had died away, replaced by cries of anger and pain carried on the chill night breeze. Bridgford strained his ears, trying to make out what was happening, but the distance was too great. Of one thing he was certain: the shots came from the direction of the rebel encampment at Montgomery's Tavern. Bridgford feared the worst and silently said a prayer for his impetuous friend, Robert Moodie. But he couldn't waste time worrying about what might have happened. His mission was too important. Bridgford and his companions kicked their horses into action once more.

Though good friends, Robert Moodie and David Bridgford were opposites in many ways. Moodie was the product of a privileged British upbringing, while Bridgford was a colonial, born in New York City in 1791 and coming to Canada six years later with his mother, Sarah, and stepfather, Robert Marsh (his birth father, Robert Bridgford, had been a captain of a commercial schooner and had been murdered during a robbery a few years prior). Moodie was a regular army officer, while Bridgford was a product of the militia system. Moodie was more impetuous and emotional, whereas Bridgford was more tempered and thoughtful. But despite their differences, both men were linked by a devotion to the British Crown and a long tradition of proud military service.[6]

For Bridgford, that service began during the War of 1812

when, as a young lad of twenty-one, he had eagerly enlisted in the militia and saw action at the siege of Detroit and several skirmishes along the Niagara Frontier. His enthusiasm for war was sobered somewhat by his experiences at the Battle of York, where he was badly wounded in combat and saw Toronto—so close to home—captured and looted by American forces. It was his first real taste of defeat, and the experience shaped him as an officer, making him more cautious. When the war ended, Bridgford had risen to the rank of colonel in command of volunteers.

In the aftermath of war, Bridgford became one of the leading citizens of Richmond Hill. He operated the first hotel in town, was a successful farmer and President of the Richmond Hill Agricultural Society, and in 1824 founded Lodge #23 of the Masonic Order. Bridgford also took a keen interest in civic affairs, serving as Magistrate of the County of York and a long-time member of Vaughan Township Council, rising to become Reeve. As a man of uncompromising principle, a leading player in Tory politics in York County, and a firm supporter of the Family Compact, it was only a matter of time before he ran afoul of Mackenzie's rebel movement.

That time came on December 4, 1837, even before the hostile crowd had gathered at Moodie's home and threatened his life. Early that afternoon, troublesome reports began to circulate of disturbances along Yonge Street: acts of vandalism, threats made by armed men toward loyalists, and traffic being stopped at gunpoint by mysterious forces. No one knew exactly what to make of it, but many believed they were signs that the gathering storm clouds of rebellion were about to break. Bridgford decided to be certain. Mounting a horse, he rode off to investigate.

Bridgford hadn't gone far before several armed men stepped out from bushes alongside the road, and with muskets leveled commanded him to dismount. He reluctantly complied and was taken prisoner. Bridgford was recognized as an important loyalist and many rebels wanted to throw him in shackles and hold him indefinitely, lest he inform authorities of what he had seen. Some few even went further, threatening violence. However, Samuel Lount, one of the rebel leaders and an old friend, intervened on Bridgford's behalf. He released the colonel on the condition that he head directly home and remain there until the crisis had passed.

Bridgford gave his word, but it was a promise he had no intention of keeping. As soon as the rebels had moved on, he snuck over to the home of Colonel Robert Moodie to plan a course of action. There they decided to ride south and warn the government about the approaching rebel army. That decision of a few hours earlier had led to his current situation, feeling his way through the darkened woods somewhere east of Montgomery's Tavern, worried about the safety of his friend Moodie, and desperately hoping to avoid rebel outposts.

After what seemed like an eternity, Bridgford directed

his horse back toward Yonge Street and cautiously coaxed it onto the muddy road. His eyes bored into the night, searching for rebel sentries. When none were found, he deemed it safe and raced south toward Toronto. Eventually, he reached Government House and roused Governor Bond Head and Colonel Fitzgibbon from their sleep, warning them that an attack upon the city was imminent.

Though weary from his ride, Bridgford's night was not yet over. Bond Head directed him to have every bell in every church tower across Toronto rung, alerting citizens to the danger and summoning militiamen to duty. The dutiful soldier eagerly complied. Then, though Bridgford had not slept for almost twenty-four hours, he was asked by Fitzgibbon to retrace his steps and return to the north to raise militia there for service against the enemy. Once again, Bridgford accepted the duty.

His luck, which had seen him avoid imprisonment a day earlier and evade rebel outposts later that night, finally ran out. The change in fortune nearly cost him his life. While riding north to rally volunteers, Bridgford stumbled into a rebel patrol and once again was taken captive at gunpoint. This time, however, the rebels were in a far more hostile mood than they had been yesterday. They knew Bridgford had alerted the government of their plan to attack and, driven in equal measure by anger over his actions and fear of the inevitable government retribution, many wanted to string him up by a rope and hang him as a spy. William Lyon Mackenzie, red-faced with barely controlled anger, was among those advocating execution. A lump formed in Bridgford's throat as he faced the possibility of a grim death by hanging.

The rope was being prepared and captors were searching for a suitable tree when David Gibson, one of the more influential rebels and a man of great moral courage, arrived on the scene. He was horrified by what he found. Participating in revolution was one thing, he argued, but murder was something else entirely and he would not be a party to it. Slowly, reluctantly, the would-be hangmen saw the wisdom of his words and gave up the idea of executing Bridgford. One by one, they walked away. Mackenzie, publicly humiliated, stormed off. Unlike the day before, however, Bridgford was not released this time. Instead, he was secured within Montgomery's Tavern with other loyalists who had been rounded up.

The matter of Bridgford's execution was not yet resolved, however. By Tuesday, December 6, Mackenzie was clearly becoming unglued as his plans unraveled and the rebel position seemed to weaken by the hour. Raging over successive setbacks, he once again decided to execute Bridgford. This time, Gibson could not dissuade Mackenzie, who ordered that the captive would be shot by firing squad the following afternoon. As it turned out, Mackenzie could not see his plan through.

Imprisoned in Montgomery's Tavern, Bridgford had a front-row seat to the battle on the morning of December 7 that not only decided the rebellion but also spared him from execution. From a window, he watched as cannon and musketry erupted around the building, and smiled when William Lyon Mackenzie was forced to flee for his life as his army was routed and his dreams for an Upper Canada republic collapsed.

Bridgford emerged from the rebellion a hero. Though many acknowledged that Colonel Moodie had sacrificed his life in service to Queen and Country, and paid respect accordingly, it was Bridgford who had succeeded where Moodie had failed in alerting the government to the impending rebel assault. Thus forewarned, Governor Bond Head was able to prepare a hasty defence that stopped the rebel advance and, two days later, defeated William Lyon Mackenzie at the Battle of Montgomery's Tavern.

Bridgford had saved Toronto, and perhaps even the province. He remained proud of that distinction until his death thirty-one years later in 1868, and never showed any resentment that his role in the Rebellion was overshadowed by that of his friend, the ill-fated Colonel Moodie.

Chapter 4:
Hotels in the Rebellion

Inns were buildings of extreme importance to early Ontario settlements, ranking ahead of even churches, schools, and general stores. They provided a place for social gatherings, public meetings, entertainment, and even trials and church sermons in lieu of more appropriate locales. Both literally, because they were generally situated in the center of the community, and figuratively village inns were the heart of the community.

Inns were also at the heart of the 1837 Mackenzie Rebellion. In fact, many of the key events surrounding the ill-fated uprising against the conservative ruling clique took place at one tavern or another. Revolutionary meetings were held in the smoky haze and plans for rebellion were hatched over drinks at bars; when the fighting erupted, rebels rallied at inns along the entire length of Yonge Street before marching on the hated government; and the main battle of the rebellion was fought at Montgomery's Tavern in what is now Toronto.

And yet, while inns were clearly central to the unfolding saga, few nineteenth-century observers had good things to say about them. In fact, most contemporary accounts were extremely critical of them. John Howison, for example, wrote that "most of the taverns of Upper Canada are indeed a burlesque upon what they profess to be. A tolerable meal can scarcely be procured at any of them."[1] They certainly did not offer the comfort, refinement and hospitality we find in modern hotels.

Nevertheless, inns were extremely popular and numerous. The reasons: cheap booze and companionship. Where else in pioneer-era Ontario could one go to gather with his friends and neighbours, share news, and complain about politics and work, while downing cheap booze?

In this atmosphere the rebellion was conceived. On February 6, 1834, dozens of citizens from across the Township of Markham gathered at Hunter's Tavern in Unionville to condemn the repeated banning of their elected representative, William Lyon Mackenzie, from the provincial legislature and to express their unequivocal support for his demand for reform. This meeting got the ball rolling toward rebellion. Technically this meeting, and the many others like it that followed, were treasonous, but few if any charges were ever laid; government officials recognized they were sitting on a powder keg and were understandably reluctant to take any steps that might set off the fuse.

The frequency of such meetings meant that taverns gained a reputation as hotbeds of radicalism, and suspicion began to fall on almost all innkeepers that they secretly supported rebellion. In actuality, their opinions on Mackenzie and his ideals varied greatly, from outward hostility on the one hand to open support on the other. But it was the perception that mattered, and as a result few tavern proprietors were unaffected by the turmoil and trauma that surrounded the uprising.

Gamble's Inn

Startled by the explosion of gunshots, the horse leaped into a run with its frightened rider ducking low against its back. Behind came several more shots, and William Lyon Mackenzie, rebel leader and one-time Mayor of Toronto, felt a bullet whiz past his ear and fly off into the night. At a dead gallop, with an unknown number of horsemen in pursuit, Mackenzie swept along Yonge Street, kicking up a cloud of snow and mud in his wake. Ahead lay Gamble's Inn. The desperate rebel guided his mare toward the establishment. Tonight, instead of drinks, Gamble's Inn would serve up Mackenzie's salvation.

The year was 1837. The exact date is unknown, lost in the mist of history. But the details of this dramatic event remain etched in local folklore, and served to elevate Nathaniel Gamble's inn from humble roadside tavern to a building of historic significance. In fact, even though the building enjoyed the distinction of being the first hotel in what is today Newmarket, and one of the first anywhere north of Toronto, it became far better known for that one brief moment of excitement in the winter of 1837 when it helped save Mackenzie from his pursuers.

Owner Nathaniel Gamble was born in 1756 to a staunchly religious Quaker family, and was still a bachelor forty-six years later when he came to Upper Canada in 1802 under the leadership of Timothy Rogers. The previous year, Rogers had applied for and received land grants for forty two-hundred-acre farms which he issued to settlers who followed him up from America. The winter of 1802 saw these land-hungry individuals, Gamble among them, heading north from Toronto by foot, trudging through "the foulest weather imaginable" to reach their new homes. Gamble settled along the west side of Yonge Street and on the south side of what would later be called Mulock Drive. This was the core of the village of Armitage, the first community in King Township and today fully engulfed by the city of Newmarket. Here he established a farm, built a hotel called Gamble's Inn, married Susannah Mercer in 1803, and raised eight children. Life was good.[2]

Gamble's Inn was a two-storey, plank-sided building with perhaps half a dozen rooms and a large barroom. It was the only licensed hotel in King Township from 1800 to 1811 and, lacking competition of any kind, became an extremely popular watering hole. Weary travelers heading north to the Lake Simcoe port of Holland Landing would often stop here, and it was a frequent stop for stage coaches once they began to appear in the late 1820s. It's also rumoured that Sir John Franklin, the great but ill-fated Arctic explorer, may have sought respite here on the initial stages of one of his journeys of discovery.

Gamble's Inn was also the social heart of the village of Armitage, and indeed of King Township as a whole.[3] The first public meeting of the Township of King was held at the hotel on March 6, 1809, and such meetings would continue to be held here exclusively until 1839. It was also the location for the first Masonic Lodge meeting north of Toronto, held in 1817, and for others thereafter. Though it hosted all manner of public forums, no gatherings of people advocating rebellion ever assembled here. Gamble simply wouldn't allow it.

And why would he? As a Quaker, his moral beliefs leaned toward peaceful resolutions to conflict and he would have looked upon rebellion as dangerous, perhaps even unlawful. And as a remarkably successful businessman, he

A typical inn of the period would have looked like this.

had no axe to grind against the government and its policies. Canada had done well by him, he was prospering thanks to government-issued liquor licences, and he was in good standing with influential individuals through his association with the Masonic Lodge. Nathaniel Gamble had no reason to support rebellion, and in fact had a great deal to lose. As a result, he distanced himself from anyone with revolutionary tendencies so that no suspicion would ever fall upon him and, when fighting broke out in December of 1837, he remained firmly on the sidelines.

Unfortunately, William Lyon Mackenzie, the rebellion's ill-fated leader, literally brought the war to his doorstep and, in the process, almost succeeded in unraveling Gamble's carefully constructed position of neutrality.

Mackenzie had expected to ride down Yonge Street as the conquering hero, leading his army of farmers and craftsmen to victory. Instead, after the disastrous Battle of Montgomery's Tavern, he found himself a fugitive on the run, spending nights hidden in dark attics or barns. It was hardly the way he had envisioned events turning out.

With posses searching the province for the rebel leader, it was perhaps just a matter of time before he was located. Hundreds of militia tramped through the woods and searched every home and barn, but always Mackenzie managed to stay one step ahead and avoid capture. The exertion was beginning to take a toll on him, however. Sleepless nights and fatigue ate away at him, and the weather was miserable, so the fugitive often found himself shivering uncontrollably while hiding and running. As days turned into weeks, hunger and exposure increasingly forced him out of the woods to seek the hospitality of sympathizers, which put both himself and his host in danger.

It was his undoing. A few weeks after the rebellion had been crushed, Mackenzie took shelter on a particularly cold night with an Armitage-area family. An observant neighbour had noticed the strange comings and goings and tipped off the loyalist militia, who converged on the farmhouse to apprehend the fugitive. Mackenzie's luck held, however. Alerted just in time of the approaching soldiers, he raced from the home, vaulted atop a horse, and kicked the animal into a gallop. The soldiers opened fire, but none struck their target. They then jumped onto their own horses and gave chase, racing north along the snow- and mud-caked Yonge Street.

More shots echoed through the still night. Splinters suddenly exploded from a low-hanging tree branch near Mackenzie's head. He jerked around to look behind and saw the pursuers rapidly gaining. Mackenzie's jaw tightened. He bent low over the saddle, riding hell-bent with bullets flying uncomfortably close to his head and more than a dozen vengeance-seeking men on his trail. Mackenzie guided his horse directly toward Gamble's Inn. The building loomed directly ahead, and still Mackenzie rode on. Desperate to escape his pursuers, he rode right through the front door and into the barroom, scattering startled patrons and tables. Nathaniel Gamble, leaning upon the bar, could only watch in stunned silence as Mackenzie, without so much as an apology, rode past at full speed, right through the building and out its rear door.

The pursuing militiamen were taken aback by the unorthodox manoeuvre. Some pulled up short of the building, unwilling to follow their prey inside. Others did give chase through the building, but slowed as their horses entered the barroom, more careful than their prey not to injure patrons or damage furnishings. Either way, the desperate move had bought Mackenzie a few vital seconds, enough to make his escape into the nearby woods.

In the coming weeks, he made his way toward the United States, where he remained in exile for many years. Unfortunately, Mackenzie had unintentionally cast Gamble's Inn in the spotlight and some began to suspect that perhaps the fugitive had sought shelter here, or that Gamble somehow aided and abetted his escape. The fact that there was absolutely no evidence to support these claims did not prevent the rumours from spreading.

Even after the stories were revealed to be no more than fiction, Gamble's Inn could not escape its association with the trauma and turmoil of Mackenzie's Rebellion. It was forever branded by its single fleeting involvement in the saga, something its owners were never comfortable with. Reflecting on the story today, Mackenzie's barroom escape seems little more than an entertaining piece of local folklore. But remember that the uprising split Upper Canada apart, pitting neighbour against neighbour, and consequently the wounds of that troubled time were very slow in healing. Any reminder of the rebellion was bound to stir up old animosities or resentments.

Unfortunately for the Gambles, they and their inn were forever linked to a rebellion they had worked so hard to remain distant from. It's no surprise that the Gambles rued the day William Lyon Mackenzie rode through their establishment and into local legend.

Milbourne's Hotel

Like the Gambles, Thornhill hotel-keeper Joseph Milbourne (sometimes spelled Milburne) had refused to participate in the rebellion, even though many of his patrons and friends took up arms and urged him to follow suit. However, unlike the Gambles, who survived the unrest and its aftermath relatively unscathed, Milbourne found his dreams shattered by it.

Milbourne had arrived in the village just south of Richmond Hill in the late 1820s and in 1829 opened a hotel on the east side of Yonge Street opposite John Street. A Quaker of English descent, he was described as a "fine, manly fellow" and a highly religious individual of strict morals.[4] In some ways, the decision to open an inn seems an odd choice in light of his strongly held beliefs. After all, throughout the early nineteenth century, Upper Canada's inns were notorious for being dens of drunkenness, violence, and uncivilized behavior. Far from resembling anything we'd consider a place of hospitality, they were generally crude and supported by the sale of alcohol in their barrooms. Yet Milbourne didn't seem at all concerned that operating an inn would jeopardize his morals, and took to his role as proprietor with enthusiasm and pride.

Milbourne's Hotel boasted two or three bedrooms (in those days, guests would often pile five or six into a room), meal service, and perhaps unsurprisingly, a bar that occupied the entirety of the ground floor. Like so many across

Ontario at the time, the inn became a hotbed of revolutionary turbulence. Stirring speeches by visiting agitators roused the excitement of drunken patrons, heated debates over government policies erupted on a nightly basis, and secretive meetings plotted the overthrow of the government.[5]

Milbourne wasn't overly troubled by any of this; it was just talk, after all, a harmless way of blowing off steam. He never actually believed it would come to rebellion, and besides, turning a blind eye toward these activities was good for business. In fact, it seemed as people grew increasingly agitated about the slow pace of reform and the more they wanted to gather to discuss the state of affairs, the better business became.

By 1837, Joseph Milbourne was comfortably wealthy. But despite his success, somewhere along the way Milbourne became disenchanted with the ruling Family Compact and began to support change. Whether he was wronged in some manner, was swayed by talk overheard in his bar, or was simply a principled man we'll never know. But what's certain is that with each passing year Milbourne grew to resent the inequalities in Upper Canada society.

And yet, while he supported the concept of change, he could not condone violence in the name of change. He would have preferred peaceful political reform and was dismayed when the failure of such means increasingly gave way to talk of armed rebellion. As the concept of an uprising gradually took on a life of its own, with loyalists and reformers taking hard-line stances against one another, Milbourne knew he would eventually have to make a decision: would he put aside his aversion to violence and side with the rebels, or would his distaste for their methods cause him to turn his back on them and his dream for a more equitable society?

The time to make a decision arrived in the summer of 1837, when he was approached by rebel leaders and asked to hide within his inn spears that had been made at Samuel Lount's forge in Holland Landing. These weapons, dozens in number, would be brought out on the eve of the uprising and used to arm the rebels in their fight against their oppressors. Milbourne considered the request for a few moments, weighing his options before flatly refusing. By hiding weapons he would be committing treason, acting against the Crown, and he couldn't bring himself to do that.

When in December the simmering resentment finally boiled over into rebellion and armed men appeared at his doorstep asking him to join their cause, Milbourne refused. He would allow them to warm themselves by the fire, and would even serve them whiskey to fortify themselves against the cold, but he was not about to lose everything he valued—his honour, his business, perhaps even his freedom or his life—in what he considered a rash, foolhardy venture.

A few days later, shortly after the rebel army was crushed at Montgomery's Tavern and the uprising defeated before it had even really begun, Milbourne was shocked to see grim-faced soldiers bursting through his door and piling into the barroom. Commotion filled the room. Some patrons looked on in stunned silence while others scurried out of the way, throwing aside chairs to steer clear of the armed men. The soldiers brought muskets to their shoulders and pushed forward, yelling at the patrons to stay back. Milbourne stepped out from behind the bar and demanded to know what was going on.

Muskets swung toward him and aimed directly at the center of his chest. "Joseph Milbourne," said an officer with obvious contempt in his voice, "in the name of the Queen, you are hereby under arrest for treason."

Milbourne had no choice but to allow himself to be led away. He spent eight miserable months in prison before he even saw the inside of a courtroom and stood before a judge. There, he was stunned to hear that he, along with ninety-one other suspected rebel sympathizers, were to be banished to the prison colony of Van Diemen's Land off the coast of Australia (now the island of Tasmania). His only crime had been to own a hotel in which people voiced their displeasure at the government and its policies; it was guilt by association. The sentence was grossly unjust, but the atmosphere in the aftermath of the rebellion was heavily laced with fear and a desire for retribution. Clearly the hotel was a nest of revolutionary vipers, the government reasoned, and its owner the most poisonous of the bunch. Milbourne would have to be punished.

Thankfully, even in those troubled days when revenge hung heavy in the air, not everyone was out for blood. Milbourne, along with all the others rounded up in the days and weeks after the Battle of Montgomery's Tavern, were pardoned on the occasion of Queen Victoria's coronation in 1838. Unfortunately, a dark cloud still hung over Milbourne and upon his return home he found it impossible to pick up the pieces of his old life. Resentment toward the rebels of 1837, or those even suspected of sympathizing with them, still lingered and as a result he found it impossible to acquire a new licence to operate the hotel. Milbourne was heartbroken. He had been thrown in jail, his loyalty questioned, he had almost been exiled to a foreign land away from his family, and now his livelihood was being taken from him. Though Milbourne pursued every avenue to recover his inn or at least secure compensation for his loss, it was to no avail.[6]

Shattered both financially and emotionally, he admitted defeat and turned his back on Thornhill. Milbourne drifted away to enter the tannery trade, but never again found the prosperity he enjoyed as a hotel-keeper in Thornhill. In many ways, though he took no part in the fighting, Joseph Milbourne was a casualty of the rebellion. The wounds of his unjust treatment never fully healed and he died a bitter man.

Chapter 5:
Chief Yellowhead and Natives

The sky was deep blue-black and heavy with clouds that held snow, giving the day the harshest and most bone-chilling feel. Doors and windows were closed and securely barred. Families huddled in their homes, hearts trembling with fear. Guns and improvised weapons were held unsteadily in sweaty, shaking hands in case of the need to defend one's home. All was eerily silent.

A few brave souls peeked out from their homes to watch with wide eyes as an army of grim-faced Indian braves, fiercely painted for war, marched confidently down Yonge Street. They carried razor-sharp tomahawks and held rifles ready in their arms. The warriors looked prepared to unleash themselves in a fury at a moment's notice.

It was December of 1837, the Rebellion of Upper Canada was well underway, and the Ojibwa Indians were on the warpath. The question on everyone's lips: who would bear the brunt of their wrath—loyalist or rebel?

The Indians of Upper Canada were largely misunderstood by white settlers. Those settlers who came from the United States (and there were many, perhaps as much as a quarter of the population) were raised on exaggerated stories of Indian savagery. Some of the older among them may even have remembered the brutal fighting that had periodically erupted along the American frontier during the latter years of the eighteenth century, as the colonies expanded west and settlers moved into Indian lands. American-born residents of Upper Canada associated Indians with blood-curdling war cries, scalping, and devastating raids upon isolated farmsteads that left trails of blood and smoke in their wake. To them, Indians were barbarians, never mind that Americans were equally guilty of barbaric acts during these conflicts.

British or Canadian-born residents didn't have the same instinctual fears of their native neighbours, largely because there had been little in the way of conflict between them. In general, the two cultures co-existed peaceably. Nevertheless, Indians represented an alien culture, and one could well imagine that newcomers fresh from the green fields of Ireland or the urban sprawl of London would have been utterly terrified by the sight of armed Indian warriors marching through their communities, their intentions and destination unknown.

Yet, they needn't have worried. The focus of the Ojibwa warriors' deadly intent was not helpless citizens but rather the rebel army of William Lyon Mackenzie. And leading them was Chief Yellowhead, one of the most loyal subjects within the vast expanse of the British Empire.

William Yellowhead, or Musquakie in his native language, was born sometime around 1765.[1] His father, also called Yellowhead by the British, was an important chief among the Ojibwa, a tribe who inhabited most of central and northern Ontario and who since the seventeenth century had cultivated close ties with Europeans.

During the War of 1812, the elder Yellowhead had ensured that the Ojibwa remained loyal to the British. In fact, many warriors fought bravely against the American invaders, standing shoulder-to-shoulder with English soldiers and Canadian militiamen. Both Yellowheads, father and son, were present at the Battle of York in 1813, during which the aging chief was severely wounded.[2] As a result, Musquakie was thrust into a leadership role, assuming the position of head chief of the Ojibwas around Lakes Simcoe and Huron.

If Yellowhead had thought his people's service and sacrifice would be rewarded in the post-war years by a grateful government, he was sadly mistaken. He wasn't expecting medals or special treatment, but simply recognition of their land claim. It didn't work out that way. In 1818, the Ojibwa chiefs were compelled to surrender 1,592,000 acres of land (comprising modern-day Grey, Wellington, Dufferin, and Simcoe counties) in exchange for the annual payment of a mere £1,200. Then, in 1830, they were persuaded to give up their migratory lifestyle and settle on land at The Narrows between lakes Couchiching and Simcoe at the site of present-day Orillia. The government built homes, a meeting house, and other structures, and hired white settlers to teach them farming. The Ojibwa proved extremely adaptable and willing to embrace their new role; an 1835 report by Indian agent Thomas Gummersall Anderson suggested they had made a successful transition from hunting to farming, and that religion and education were increasingly important in their lives.[3]

Then Lieutenant-Governor Sir Francis Bond Head entered the picture. The agent's report meant nothing to him; the wishes of the Ojibwa meant even less. What he wanted was to open up even more land to British settlers, lands then occupied by the Ojibwa. As a result, he ordered Yellowhead's people to once again uproot and start their lives over again at a reserve at Rama. As before, the loyal Ojibwa quietly obliged.

Despite the constant upheavals and deception, and the fact that they were excluded from most areas of politics and the economy, the Ojibwa remained steadfast in their loyalty to the Crown. They had fought bravely for the British during the War of 1812, and were determined to do so again in 1837. When word of the rebellion reached Rama, Chief Yellowhead called a council where he announced his intention to go to the aid of the government. Despite his people's mistreatment over the years he felt compelled to go to the aid of the British. There were dissenting voices amongst the Ojibwa, however. They had been uprooted several times, forced to give up their traditional lifestyle and adapt to European ways, yet were excluded from most aspects of society. Why should they lend their support to the government? Yellowhead argued that it was a matter of duty and honour, and eventually won over his people. And so he and his followers hurriedly donned war paint, grabbed their weapons, and raced for the scene of action.

The force Yellowhead commanded probably numbered between fifty and one hundred warriors, not a particularly large but certainly a potent force. During the War of 1812, Indians had proven so intimidating that the mere sight of them had caused veteran American soldiers to panic, and on more than one occasion hardened commanders surrendered to British officers to spare themselves from "the savages."[4] Imagine then the psychological effect they would have had upon the untrained farmers and craftsmen that composed Mackenzie's army.

By the time Chief Yellowhead and his men reached Toronto, the Battle of Montgomery's Tavern had been fought and won, the rebel army shattered and its leaders in hiding. Nevertheless, Yellowhead's warriors helped ensure that there was little subsequent violence or attempt to rebuild the shattered rebel army. Their presence alone caused people to think twice before continuing the struggle.

Yet the atmosphere in the colony remained tense. Mackenzie was attempting to reignite the flames of rebellion from the safety of the United States, where he and his men enjoyed considerable popular support. At the same time, armed rebels remained at large, prowling the back roads and woods of Upper Canada, and many communities remained unsettled.

Among these villages in turmoil were Bradford, Holland Landing and Sharon, from which many of the most radical rebels had originated. Lieutenant-Governor Bond Head, worried that this simmering resentment would once again boil over into violence, requested that Chief Yellowhead and his band spend the winter encamped at Holland Landing to keep a watchful eye on events there. Should there be any unrest, they were to stamp it out immediately.

There was another, equally important reason for Bond Head to ask the Ojibwa to overwinter here. At the time, Holland Landing served as a port for shipping across Lake Simcoe and a link in the vital route from Toronto to the military base at Penetanguishene, on Georgian Bay—a strategic and economic necessity. Any interruption in the flow of traffic along this route would have grave repercussions, and it was with an eye toward that possibility as much as the threat from discontent in the communities of the region that Chief Yellowhead and his warriors were posted to Holland Landing.

Life in the hastily established camp was a miserable experience, and the Ojibwa faced considerable hardships over the harsh months that followed. They were unable to do their winter hunting, so were reliant upon the government to tend to their needs. However, pay and provisions suddenly stopped arriving after only a few weeks, leaving the Indians in dire straits as food ran desperately short. Though a proud man, Yellowhead was forced to petition the government for supplies, claiming that his people were at risk of starvation unless they got immediate relief. Finally, food began to arrive and the immediate danger passed, but the combination of biting cold and utter boredom made for a dreadful existence.

Come spring, Chief Yellowhead and his warriors returned to Rama with the thanks of a grateful British government. They had done their duty and made a valuable contribution to maintaining the peace and security of Upper Canada, but the Indians were understandably eager to return to their families.

Despite the fact that the rebellion was viewed by most Indians as a white man's dispute in which they had little direct interest, other Indian tribes played a role in the fighting as well. For example, as many as one hundred Six Nations men from Grand River volunteered to serve under

William Johnson Kerr alongside the militia in the Hamilton region. On December 14, these warriors saw action against a handful of rebels near the village of Sodom, killing at least three of them.[5]

The contribution of the Indian warriors in 1837 and 1838 was the last occasion in which tribal allies served directly with the British in the defence of Canada. In what amounted to a farewell salute, the Crown expressed its gratitude in a statement before parliament, and by representatives of the Crown to Objibwa themselves for "their faithful and honourable conduct while engaged in Her Majesty's Military Service."

Mackenzie's Rebellion was the last time William Yellowhead was called upon to take up weapons. He had done his share for King and Country, and lived the rest of his life in peace. After returning from a winter hunting trip in 1864, the venerable chief suddenly took ill with pneumonia and died. At the time, he was thought to be upwards of one hundred years of age, although the burial register at St. James Church, Orillia, lists his age as ninety-five. Despite serving bravely in two conflicts, he was a man of peace and so it was appropriate that he died in bed at an advanced age. A large gathering of settlers and Indians attended Chief Yellowhead's funeral out of respect for this influential chief who always demonstrated loyalty to the British crown. Even, some might hasten to add, when loyalty wasn't always returned in kind.

Chapter 6:
Outlaws and Villains

In the eyes of the British government and loyal citizens of Upper Canada, every man who took up arms in support of William Lyon Mackenzie or gave aid to the cause was an outlaw and villain. Such men had committed the most terrible of crimes: that of treason. There could be no justification for attempting to overthrow the rightful government, regardless of the grievances, and therefore these men were viewed with absolute disdain by most of their friends and neighbours.

But there were men amongst the rebel ranks who more properly fit the terms outlaw and villain, individuals who made a career out of committing crimes and who continued their unlawful ways even years after the rebellion had been defeated. These men bore more resemblance to the violent brigands of the American West than to the desperate farmers and idealistic townsfolk who made up most of the rebel army; hateful and brutal, they had no respect for the rule of law and existed in the shadowy fringes of society.

The two most notorious of this unsavoury bunch were Henry Johnson, leader of Ontario's first criminal organization, and Benjamin Lett, a terrorist whose path of mayhem and bloodshed saw him labelled Public Enemy Number One.

Henry Johnson

In the sweltering summer heat of 1846 in the provincial capital of Toronto, the leader of the notorious mob of thieves known as the Markham Gang was finally brought to justice.[1] The criminal stared viciously at the judge as the verdict was announced before the courtroom overflowing with curious onlookers. He cracked the knuckles of one chain-bound hand with his other. It was a thinly veiled threat, announcing to the judge and jury that Johnson intended to get his revenge. He was a man used to intimidating his enemies, and watched with silent satisfaction as the judge began to shift uncomfortably in his chair. But nothing could change that fact that it was prison for Henry Johnson, and in towns and villages across Ontario people rejoiced.

For good reason: at the head of the Markham Gang, the earliest organized crime cartel in Ontario, Henry Johnson had cut a heartless path of theft and lawlessness across the province through the late 1830s and 1840s. Most people thought he didn't have a decent bone in his body, and they were probably right.

It was said at the time that he was marked for evil by his devilish appearance: "black complexion, black hair, and black eyes."[2] Though of only medium height and build, there was something intimidating about him, a coldness about his eyes that set people aback, and he was well-known for having a hair-trigger temper that could erupt into violence seemingly in the blink of an eye.

It wasn't as if Johnson could claim his criminal ways were the result of a broken home or heartbreaking poverty. Born in 1819, he was raised in a loving environment by his staunchly religious and law-abiding father, Cornelius Johnson. A farmer with extensive holdings in Pickering and Markham, Cornelius ensured that his children did not want for much. In fact, their futures were all but secured by the properties they were bound to inherit, so there was little apparent motive for Henry Johnson's depraved behavior.

If one looked a little deeper, one would discover that the seeds of Johnson's lawless ways were sown during William Lyon Mackenzie's ill-fated 1837 rebellion, and took root while Johnson languished in prison with hardened criminals afterwards.

At the time, most economic and political clout in Ontario lay in the hands of aristocratic families collectively known as the Family Compact. In order to have any real rights in nineteenth-century Ontario, one had to be English, well-bred and wealthy, and Anglican. Everyone else existed in varying degrees of irrelevance, including the Johnson family, who were Methodist and of American descent. Throughout the 1820s and early 1830s there was a growing swell of discontentment against such prejudice, yet the conserva-tive Family Compact would hear nothing of reform. When it became apparent that peaceful change was not going to come about, many decided violent action was necessary to achieve that end. Eighteen-year old Henry Johnson was among those willing to take up arms in the cause of liberty.

Johnson was fortunate enough to survive without injury the fifteen minutes of fighting at Montgomery's Tavern that decided the rebellion, but was captured shortly thereafter and was forced to endure many gruelling months of tortured exist-ence in a cold prison cell with poor food and terrible sanita-tion. When he emerged a year later, he was a changed man, a cynical man. He had decided he owed the world nothing. What he wanted he would take, and he gathered around him other shady and ruthless individuals to form the Markham Gang.

The Markham Gang had its roots in the secretive societies that had covertly met to plot rebellion in the years leading up to 1837. In fact, many gang members had been active within these outlawed political groups, where they established a wide network of informants and allies, learned how to organize and plan illegal activities, and developed skills at avoiding the interest of authorities. Now, the former rebels simply put these assets to new use as thieves.

While their crimes were focused in Toronto, Markham Township, King Township, East Gwillimbury, Whitchurch, and the Brock and Newcastle districts, the tentacles of the Markham Gang (also known as the Swamp Gang and the Markham Black Hand Gang) reached across the entirety of the province and even into Quebec and the United States. Horses, money, rifles, tools—Johnson and his partners in crime knew no limits to their thievery. Any resistance they encountered was met with raw, unfeeling brutality.

One of the most ruthless members of the gang, Johnson was among its leaders (the *British Colonist* went so far as to refer to him as the group's "director," implying he was the kingpin of the entire criminal operation).[3] For years, he worked on his father's farm by day and moonlighted with his fellow thieves. His specialty was burglary; under the cover of darkness, he would slip into a home and soundlessly make off with valuables, often with the family sleeping just an arm's length away, oblivious to the invasion. Planning was the key to his success. Before he robbed a building Johnson ensured he knew exactly where valuables were kept, thereby limiting the chance of detection and ensuring the greatest reward for the risk. To obtain this vital information he would carefully case a home and its inhabitants for days or weeks, and oftentimes bribed or threatened household servants.

Johnson's wild ways seem to have been known by the law for quite some time, but there was never enough evidence to convict him of any felony. Part of the reason for his elusiveness was the secretive, insular nature of the Markham Gang. Members made solemn vows never to speak about their crimes, accepting that should they turn informer they would end up dead and buried in some out-of-the way location. Even if death stared them in the face, they would not give up their secrets. The Markham Gang took their crimes and their rules very seriously. Bonds between members were made all the stronger by the intermarriage that took place between them; your partner in crime might very well also be your brother-in-law. As a result, to turn on a gang member was to turn on family, and that just wasn't done.

Intimidation also helped keep Johnson free. Victims and witnesses were terrified to go to the authorities because they were deathly afraid of the repercussions. To speak out against Henry Johnson was to invite a beating, the burning of your home or business, even murder. Understandably, no one was willing to step forward to point an accusing finger Johnson's way, and as a result he evaded the long arm of the law for almost a decade.

But by May 1846, things had changed. Evidence had been gathered, people had talked, deals had been struck. The

Crown finally felt they had enough proof of wrongdoings to successfully pursue a conviction.

In the early days of November 1845, six members of the Markham Gang robbed the home of John Morrow. Four were quickly arrested, but Johnson and good friend Robert Burr fled and made for southwestern Ontario. Here, far removed from Toronto, Johnson felt himself beyond the reach of the law, and perhaps became overconfident as a result. He should have lain low, to let the Morrow robbery recede from memory, but that wasn't in his nature. Instead, he and Burr continued their criminal ways. On January 10, they stole $40 worth of grain from a farm in Zorra, and later that month stole quantities of cloth, harnesses, and buffalo robes from an area business.

Local constables began to take note and were soon on Johnson's trail, doggedly following every lead in an effort to run down the elusive criminal. Luck was on their side; a tip led them to a barn near Embro where Johnson and Burr were hiding with their loot.

The constables silently approached the weathered building, their pistols drawn in anticipation of resistance. When they burst through the doors, they found their prey completely startled and unprepared to either fight or flee. Their weapons were out of reach, and they had no way of making a desperate run for freedom. Johnson was a trouble-hunting man, and he wasn't about to go easily. He stared hard at the constables, thinking to intimidate them as he inched closer to his pistols. His eyes showed contempt for the law and those who had come here to uphold it.

But this time, perhaps for the first time in his life, he couldn't strike fear into his opponents. Instead of backing down under his baleful glare, they stepped closer and their guns never wavered. "Give yourself up," one of the lawmen said coldly and firmly. He was determined, calm, confident. Johnson knew in that instant he had no choice but to do as he was ordered. He raised his arms in reluctant surrender.

For the second time in his life, he was cast in chains and shipped to Toronto to stand trial. The principal witness for the prosecution was Casper Stotts, one of the thieves originally arrested for the robbery, who in order to save his own hide agreed to reveal the secrets of the Markham Gang and testify against his former mate. He knew that traitors were threatened with death, but cutting a deal was the only way he could avoid a lengthy prison term. It was a dangerous gamble, but he took it nonetheless.

Johnson was charged with petty theft, burglary, robbery, assault, and horse rustling. Thanks to Stotts's damning testimony, he was convicted of all charges and sentenced to four years in Kingston Penitentiary. The verdict was greeted with expressions of relief across the province. The *Brockville Reporter* on November 12, 1846, noted: "Our readers will be pleased to hear that another of the most formidable and dangerous of this notorious gang has been brought to justice."[4]

Many other members of the Markham Gang were arrested, tried, and incarcerated at the same time. Deprived of its leadership, the bonds that had held it so firmly together were broken, its secrets out; the Markham Gang was shattered. Its power was broken for good, and upon their release from prison the one-time outlaws took up honest pursuits.

Henry Johnson was no different. When he was released in 1850, he was once again a changed man. It seems the chip on his shoulder was gone and he had resolved to lead an honest existence. Indeed, he made every effort to conceal his criminal past and became a thoroughly law-abiding citizen. He settled on one of his father's properties in Markham Township and focused his energies toward agricultural pursuits. Proving to be a capable farmer, Johnson added even more land to his estate over the years, including extensive holdings in Stouffville. It was to these properties that he moved in the 1860s, in an attempt perhaps to escape the dark cloud of his criminal past. In light of his earlier record, it's perhaps ironic that his son, Hiram Henry Johnson, became a prominent banker in Stouffville and the community's first Reeve.[5]

Henry Johnson died in Stouffville on June 2, 1895, and was buried in Dickson Hill cemetery. He was mourned as a good neighbour and an upstanding citizen. His wild days had been cleansed away by a term in prison and five decades of honest living. He had truly reformed his ways. Or had he? It's an interesting coincidence that in the 1860s, immediately after Johnson moved to Stouffville, that community was plagued by a gang of horse thieves. In fact, the situation grew so troublesome that a vigilante organization, the Stouffville Association for the Apprehension of Felons, had to take action to combat the wave of crime.

Had Henry Johnson been up to his old tricks? We'll never know.

Benjamin Lett

In the Niagara River, an inferno raged atop the water. A schooner, the rebel-operated *Caroline*, was ablaze and adrift in the current, being pulled downstream toward the Falls. The heat rose in searing sheets, and the roar of the flaming maelstrom carried across the still night. The burning mast fell and struck the black water, casting a weird reflection as the flames were extinguished. Dark smoke, blacker than the night, roiled from the burning vessel to hover like fog above the river's surface.

Caught in the eerie glow, seven longboats pulled quickly for the safety of the Canadian shore. All of the men aboard were filled with satisfaction that they had been successful in their mission to destroy the vessel responsible for supplying rebel forces encamped on Navy Island. It had been a daring gamble, carried out under the cover of darkness and at sword-point, but it had gone off without a hitch or injury among the attackers. More importantly, the raid had struck a serious blow to William Lyon Mackenzie's plans to continue his rebellion despite his recent defeat at Montgomery's Tavern.

On the American shore, Benjamin Lett seethed with barely concealed anger as he watched the *Caroline* burn. The sight fuelled his hatred of Britain and its loyalists in Upper Canada, fanning the flames of vengeance that blackened his soul like a dense layer of soot. One day, Lett vowed as he stalked the snow-blanketed shore, he would avenge the *Caroline.* There was no doubt in his mind that he would make good on his promise, and on that day the men responsible for the ship's destruction would pay dearly for their actions.

From that moment, Benjamin Lett began a campaign of vengeance that terrorized the Niagara region for more than a decade. A brutal outlaw who never hesitated to spill blood, Lett would arrive at a target's door at night with a pistol in one hand, knife in the other, and murder in his eyes. He was Public Enemy Number One in Canada, with a string of assassinations, bombings, and acts of sabotage to his name. The British government was desperate to bring his reign of fear to an end, one way or the other.

Lett's hatred of the British began well before the rebellion of 1837. He was born in Ireland in 1814, and some accounts suggest his mother was raped by English soldiers during the endless cycle of violence that wracked the island. We do know that this violence cost Lett his uncle, who was viciously murdered in 1798. The family moved to Canada in

1819 and settled on a farmstead just east of Toronto where, just a few short years later, Lett's father died in a tragic accident. Misfortune, which had plagued the family for so long, turned its attention elsewhere after that and for the next two decades the family lived a quiet and by all accounts contented life.

Nevertheless, there was something unsettled in Benjamin simmering beneath the surface, building to a slow boil that most observers would have agreed was eventually bound to erupt. That eruption finally occurred during the rebellion of 1837, when the angry, troubled young man was driven onto a path of murder and mayhem.

Though he had remained aloof from the fighting, Benjamin Lett was nonetheless swept up by the currents of revolution. Soon after Mackenzie's army was dispersed at the Battle of Montgomery's Tavern, a loyalist posse rode into the Lett farm and demanded that Benjamin join them in hunting down suspected rebels. The Irishman refused; while he took no part in the rebellion he sympathized with their cause and certainly felt no loyalty to Queen and Country. His refusal to assist cast suspicion upon him, and the posse arrested him. Lett seethed with anger at the injustice of it all, and dreaded the thought of spending months or even years behind bars. He had no intention of going without a fight, but rather than make a hasty attempt at escape waited patiently for an opening to present itself. Lett saw his chance while being transported to prison in Kingston, managing to overpower his guards and flee into the woods with musket balls shredding bark all around him.

Now a wanted man, Lett headed toward New York State and joined the Patriot Hunters (or simply Patriots), a group of exiled rebels who plotted the overthrow of the British in Canada. Based in New York State, they crossed the Niagara River under the cover of darkness to terrorize the population of Upper Canada. Their raids were calculated to arouse fear, disrupt commerce, and incite a war between the United States and Britain that they hoped would end with American victory and the independence of Canada. The vast majority of these raids were relatively minor, involving threatening letters, robberies, barn burnings, the slaughter of cattle, and beatings.

Some, however, were far more heinous, and invariably these carried the dark signature of Benjamin Lett. The crime that solidified Lett's reputation for extremism and brutality occurred during the night of November 16, 1838.

Lett silently slipped from shadow to shadow as he approached the Chippewa home of Captain Edgeworth Ussher, a noted British loyalist. Lett had not picked his target at random; months earlier, Captain Ussher had guided the rowboats carrying men across the Niagara River to board and burn the rebel schooner, *Caroline*. Lett reasoned that selecting this respected military man as a target for assassination, an individual hailed locally as a hero, would surely send a powerful message.

Lett may have been musing on this when a dog suddenly barked in the distance, shattering the night's stillness. He lowered himself to the ground and pressed his body flat, waiting there motionless for long moments. When the barking had stopped, he raised himself up and quickly raced the final distance to Ussher's home. There, he climbed onto the porch and disrupted the silence by rapping loudly on the door. The knocks echoed through the night, causing the dog in the distance to resume his howling.

Captain Ussher awoke at the sound. His wife, Sally, stirred beside him. Ussher lit a candle, slipped from his bed, and pulled on a robe. Sally, now alert as well, begged him not to answer the door. The string of nighttime assaults upon people and property by the hands of the Patriot Hunters had her on edge, and she knew her husband's pro-British sentiments made him a target for retribution. But Ussher would not live in fear; he would answer the door and prove he couldn't be intimidated.

There was more rapping at the door, more urgent now, as Ussher peeked in on his four children, lying fearful in their beds, blankets pulled tight to their chins. Ussher urged them back to sleep, then descended the stairs and made his way across the hall. He pulled open the door and was greeted by two shots ringing out from the blackness. Ussher caught the bullets full in his chest and fell to the ground as his shadowy assailant disappeared into the gloom. When Sally arrived

The burning of the rebel vessel Caroline *on the Niagara River was a defining moment in Benjamin Lett's life.*

at his side moments later, his eyes were glassy and his fingers twitching uncontrollably. The soon-to-be widow cried and screamed, and somewhere in the darkness of the night Benjamin Lett smiled.

Lett and his followers revelled in the perceived victory. A poem boasting of the murder, entitled "On the Execution of Captain Ussher" and probably written by the terrorist's own hand, appeared in the Lockport, New York, *Freeman's Advocate.* Here was a man who didn't just kill out of some twisted sense of duty, but more importantly because he enjoyed the notoriety and attention his exploits generated.

Ussher's assassination was not the only crime in which Lett became implicated. In January 1839 he made an unsuccessful attempt to burn a British ship at Kingston. Six months later, he was implicated in a failed raid on the town of Cobourg. This lack of success in 1839 left Lett frustrated and full of self-doubt by year's end. He needed to make a spectacular statement in 1840, something that would shake the enemy and bolster the faltering spirits of the Patriots. To do that, Lett elected to strike at what was then one of Canada's most recognizable symbols, the monument to War of 1812 hero General Isaac Brock.

Brock was a martyr, having sacrificed his life to secure victory at the Battle of Queenston Heights and save the nation from American occupation. He was Canada's first hero, an instant legend, and his remains were buried beneath a 135-foot-tall monument built atop the very bluff where he fell mortally wounded on October 12, 1812. Lett struck against this revered edifice on Good Friday, April 17, 1840. The peace and tranquility of that sacred day were shattered by rumbling echoes rolling down from atop Queenston Heights, and when people went to investigate they found the Brock Monument defiled. A powerful bomb had exploded inside the base of the memorial, shattering the staircase, blowing off part of the peak and cracking the column. Canadians were outraged; Lett and his followers rejoiced.

Perhaps overconfident in the wake of this resounding success, Lett made a clumsy and ill-planned attempt in June to burn a steamship at Oswego, New York. Caught in the act, he was arrested, promptly convicted of arson, and sentenced to seven years of hard labour at the prison in Auburn, New York. Lett had no intention of languishing behind bars, however. En route to prison, he once again managed to break free from his guards and escape into the woods. The embarrassed and enraged Governor of New York offered a huge reward for his capture. Those attempting to apprehend him were urged to proceed with caution, since Lett was considered armed and extremely dangerous.

Lett was now wanted on both sides of the border and had no safe haven, yet he remained at large for more than a year, thanks in large part to the shelter and support provided by his rebel compatriots. It wasn't until September 1841 that he was recaptured in Buffalo, escorted to prison by a large party of heavily armed police, and thrown into the hell of solitary confinement. Here, surrounded by darkness and the scurrying of roaches, he had years on end to reflect on his violent, murderous ways. According to his brother Thomas, Lett was regularly beaten by the guards, crippling his body and spirit.

During his incarceration, the tenor of the times changed. The British government had offered amnesty to most rebels, including leaders such as William Lyon Mackenzie, and had taken steps to address most of their complaints by making extensive reforms in the political and economic realms. As a result, there was no longer any appetite for revolution and Lett's former allies distanced themselves from him and other radicals like him.

After four years behind bars Lett was pardoned by New York Governor Silas Wright. The years in prison had shattered his health and dampened his appetite for revolution, and instead of continuing his personal crusade against the British he went to live with his siblings on a farm near Northville, Illinois. There he lived in obscurity; he didn't talk much about his past and his acquaintances didn't ask a lot of questions. It was a quiet life, but it apparently suited him.

However, his violent past eventually caught up with him. In December 1858, while involved in a trading expedition on Lake Michigan, Lett suddenly became violently ill. He was raced by steamship to Milwaukee but faded quickly, and despite the doctor's best efforts died nine days later. An autopsy indicated death by strychnine poisoning. Thomas Lett and many other observers were certain that British agents were responsible for what was clearly murder.

Few mourned his passing. Benjamin Lett had been feared throughout Canada as a man willing to murder anyone who stood in his path and who revelled in sowing the seeds of chaos. To most Canadians, and especially those in Niagara, he was a despicable villain who deserved to die. While they may have preferred that he die at the end of a rope after a trial, death by poison was preferable to allowing the terrorist go free. The consensus at the time was that he got what he deserved.

Chapter 7:

The Sharon Martyrs: James Kavanagh and James Henderson

The Sharon Temple is among Ontario's most unusual and historic attractions. Located in the village of Sharon and built in 1825, this beautiful three-storey building (often described as looking like a tiered wedding cake) was the centre of worship for the Children of Peace, an offshoot of the Quaker movement.

In a twist of contradiction, the Sharon Temple was also a centre for the rebellion of 1837. While the Children of Peace hated violence, their religious beliefs stressed social equality and democracy. As a result, they were strong supporters of the reform movement and by 1837, when attempts at political change had been frustrated, many of the Children of Peace joined the ranks of the rebel army that marched down Yonge Street in an effort to overthrow Upper Canada's government.

Two of these idealistic, if perhaps naïve, men died in the brief struggle: James Kavanagh and James Henderson. They were among the very few fatalities of the rebellion, and the only two who were members of the Children of Peace. Their stories say much about the type of individuals who stood behind William Lyon Mackenzie, the grievances which led otherwise law-abiding men to take up arms against the Crown, and the nature of the ill-fated rebellion itself. Perhaps most importantly, their stories also reveal the reasons why members of this religious sect would put aside their aversion to violence and join the uprising.

Mackenzie had considerable support in the rural areas north of Toronto, especially in the region around Newmarket, Bradford, Holland Landing, and Sharon. It must be remembered that at the time this represented the frontier of Ontario. Roads were primitive, luxuries and amenities were few and far between, and most inhabitants were still struggling to establish farmsteads. Life was difficult at the best of times. To residents in this area, Toronto was a distant place and the government located there was seemingly uninterested in their welfare.

The popularity of William Lyon Mackenzie in this region

was also due in large part to the magnetism and influence of one of his chief lieutenants, Samuel Lount of Holland Landing. Lount was a blacksmith by trade but was deeply involved in politics and the reform movement. Between shoeing horses he would hold secretive meetings, speak out against the corrupt government, and forge spears in his workshop. It was he who recruited Kavanagh and Henderson into the rebel ranks, and who ultimately led them to their deaths in December of 1837.

James Kavanagh was born in 1793 in Wexford, Ireland.[1] From his early teens he was apprenticed to a cobbler, and by age eighteen was employed as a shoemaker in Dublin. Kavanagh wasn't a cobbler for long. With the war against Napoleon Bonaparte raging across Europe, the British army was in constant need of recruits to replace casualties and keep their regiments at full strength. On December 11, 1811, probably enticed by the cash bounty for enlistment, eighteen-year-old James Kavanagh joined the Ninety-ninth Regiment of Foot.

Since 1806, the Ninety-ninth Foot had been stationed in Nova Scotia as part of the garrison for British North America (as Canada was then called). Perhaps Kavanagh enlisted in that regiment in the hope of avoiding combat. We'll never know, but if that was indeed his objective, it backfired in his face: in 1812, America declared war on Britain and promptly invaded British North America. The war lasted four long years, during which the 99th—and with it James Kavanagh—saw much fighting.[2]

Kavanagh was discharged from service in 1818 when the Ninety-ninth Foot was disbanded. He received one hundred acres of land in Tecumseh Township, Simcoe County, as reward for his time in the army but was refused a military pension because he could not provide discharge papers. It seems that it was this inability to secure a pension and other benefits which eventually caused the former soldier to grow disenchanted with the colonial government.

By the eve of the rebellion, Kavanagh was living rather humbly as a shoemaker in the village of Hope (now called Sharon), the Tecumseh land apparently having not worked out. He had a wife and six children, but rented a one-storey home with a mere one-acre garden. His only possessions of note were a pair of milking cows. Clearly, he was struggling to make ends meet and badly missed the military pension that was his due. It was also clear, in light of the crop failure of 1837 and resulting recession, that he might have trouble feeding his family over the coming winter.[3]

So it was that when Samuel Lount began to march his motley army down Yonge Street in December of 1837, James Kavanagh once again found himself bearing arms. He felt he had no choice; the government had failed him and changes would have to be made quickly if he was to provide for his wife and children. While he had little interest in fighting another war—soldiering was a young man's profession, after

Rebels, including James Henderson and James Kavanagh, marching on Toronto.

all—he certainly was not about to sit idly by and watch his family starve over the winter. If rebellion was the only way he could get the government to address his needs, so be it.

As a former soldier, Kavanagh would have been one of the very few rebels with any military experience. The armed rabble to which he and James Henderson belonged possessed no uniformity in unit integrity, direction, or organization. It wasn't an army in any real sense, just a mob of disenchanted and desperate men. No one had any idea how these farmers- and craftsmen-turned-soldiers would perform in battle.

Kavanagh didn't get to see the outcome for himself. He was wounded on December 5 "by a comrade" in what presumably was an accident, probably a nervous sentry firing out of hand.[4] Kavanagh died seven days later, long enough to see the revolution he had hoped to be a part of blow away like tracks in a winter snow squall.

James Henderson shared a similar fate. Born around 1815, he joined the Children of Peace in 1836 in order to wed Ellen Hughes, a young woman belonging to a family considered among the most religious members of the sect.[5] The Hughes family also held to long-standing pacifist beliefs, dating back to the American Revolution when Ellen's grandfather, Job Hughes, was persecuted for his unwillingness to become embroiled in the conflict.[6]

James and Ellen were married on March 25, 1837, and resided in the home Ellen and her sister had inherited upon the death of their parents. Scarcely eight months later, despite the moral stance of his new wife and her family, Henderson answered William Lyon Mackenzie's call to arms.

As a young man of only twenty-two years of age, James Henderson couldn't possibly have had real grievances against the government. He hadn't been wronged in any way, hadn't seen enough of the world to witness inequalities, and hadn't lived long enough to grow bitter over failures. For him, the rebellion was an idealistic crusade and probably an adventure of sorts. After all, Mackenzie had assured his followers that it would be a bloodless victory.

Ellen didn't want him to go. She cried and begged

for him to stay with her, to not get involved, but his mind had been made up. Reform was a cause worth fighting for, Henderson assured his new bride as he pulled himself from her clinging arms. He would come back to her and together they'd raise a family in a better province. He promised. With that, he kissed her gently on the forehead and joined other rebels awaiting him by the roadside.

Henderson participated in the march down Yonge Street. The little army of farmers and craftsmen were joined at every community by eager recruits and the atmosphere was one of optimism. It appeared as though overthrowing the Family Compact would be merely a matter of marching, and it surely must have seemed to Henderson that the matter would be easily resolved, just as Mackenzie had promised.

The first skirmish occurred on December 5 at Gallows Hill, where hundreds of rebels were confronted by a small force of loyalist militia, most of whom were battle-hardened retired army officers. Suddenly the rabble of farmers and craftsmen were confronted by the dreadful reality of war. One can only assume that Henderson, a simple farmer and barely more than a boy, was frightened by the well-armed professional soldiers assembled before him.

Suddenly, the Loyalists fired a volley from their muskets that swept like a scythe running through the rebel forces, and men dropped. Several were wounded, and one had died. That lone fatality was James Henderson. His comrades scattered in headlong retreat, leaving his body lying in the muddy road alongside their collective hopes for revolution.

The *Patriot and Farmer's Monitor* newspaper reported in its December 8 edition that "near the body of the dead Rebel (Henderson) were found a fowling piece and two pikes about ten feet long, manufactured with punctilious regard to destructiveness: the blades stuck into the shafts, which are of hickory, are spear-shaped, sharply-pointed, and double-edged, calculated for thrusting and ripping up bellies, no doubt the contrivance of the bloody-minded villain, Mackenzie."[7] Though the newspaper made them sound like vicious weapons, knives and spears were hardly a match for muskets.

The deaths of James Kavanagh and James Henderson, while tragic, were not without purpose. Frightened by the outbreak of violence, the British began to reform the governance of Upper Canada and address some of the worst grievances. A better province, one which began to reflect some of the ideals held dear by the Children of Peace, did emerge from the turmoil of rebellion.

Chapter 8:

Women and Children

When one talks about war, the focus is usually on the men who fought so hard to keep their women and children safe during those horrible times. After all, traditionally, soldiering has been a male profession. But on the odd occasion, you'll also come across women and children who played important roles during wartime and who displayed incredible bravery in the face of mortal danger. Perhaps because it was played out amongst the towns and cities of Ontario, not on some distant battlefield, the Rebellion of 1837 saw several acts of heroism and sacrifice from such unlikely sources.

Women and Children

The De Grassi Girls

During the Rebellion of 1837 loyalists and rebels fought against each other with great determination, and while many of these men were civilians with little or no military training, they nonetheless gave their all to fight for what they believed was right. Not all participants in the rebellion were men, however. In fact, some of the bravest acts were performed by two heroic young girls, aged ten and thirteen, who risked their young lives to help the government by providing vital information that led to the eventual defeat of the uprising. Their actions were every bit as heroic as that performed by Laura Secord a generation earlier during the War of 1812 and yet, unlike Secord, they remain virtually unknown.

Charlotte and Cornelia De Grassi were the daughters of Filippo "Philip" De Grassi, an Italian-born soldier who served many years in the British army and eventually settled in Toronto.[1] De Grassi was born in Rome in 1793, but trained at the French military academy and served as a captain in the French Army during the Napoleonic Wars. He was captured in Portugal by the British and shipped to England, where he joined the British Army. De Grassi was then sent to the British West Indies and served there from 1812 to 1815. After his tour, he returned to England, married Charlotte Hearn, and went on to father seven children.[2]

It was around this time that he began to find it hard to support his growing family with his income as a language teacher. De Grassi was advised that a better life could be had in Canada where retired officers were being given extensive land grants for free. He decided to make a move there; in 1831, De Grassi and his family packed up their meagre belongings and headed to Canada where he settled on a two-hundred-acre farm in Toronto. He wasn't wealthy by any means and had to endure the same hardships as any other settler in the new country, but it was a fresh start and at least here he was the proud owner of land he could call his own.

We don't really know when De Grassi joined the militia in Upper Canada, but we do know he was firmly opposed to Mackenzie and his followers. In fact, he wrote his thoughts on the rebellion in his journal: "I managed amidst great trials and difficulties to struggle on until that unfortunate rebellion broke out in 1837, when Mr. W.L. Mackenzie thought to take upon himself more than legal functions and declared that my property and that of many other loyal men should be parceled out among his followers."[3]

De Grassi stood to lose everything he owned should the rebellion succeed, so it's little wonder that he would take up arms against Mackenzie and his followers. At 11 p.m. on December 5, the very night the rebellion broke out, De Grassi mounted his horse and, with his two daughters Charlotte and Cornelia in tow, went to Toronto to offer his services to the Government. Imagine two young girls in the still of the cold, eerily silent woods following their father into the unknown.

Women and Children

Cornelia (aged thirteen) and Charlotte (aged ten) were no strangers to hard work and had endured many struggles as members of a family that had to work together just to make ends meet. These young girls did not have time to enjoy their childhood, playing hop-scotch or hide-and-seek, or having the luxury of dolls to play with. The only thing these two sisters knew was the responsibility of many tiring chores. They knew what it was to churn butter until their arms ached or to peel potatoes until they could no longer feel their fingers. They were mature beyond their age, and by today's standards were young women.

But despite knowing hardship and hard work, no one could have imagined that these two young girls would play an important role in the rebellion. When most women and children remained fearful at home, watching only from the sidelines as events unfolded and the future of Upper Canada—their future—was decided, these brave girls decided to help their government in any way they could.

The dangers Cornelia and Charlotte faced riding alongside their father were many. The temperatures had dropped to a numbing coldness by the time they set out, and they feared getting lost in the black darkness of the night as they rode through thick, dense woods with branches whipping their faces. There was also the ever-present danger of being spotted by a rebel patrol; a trigger-happy rebel might be lurking behind any tree or within the dark folds of any shadow.

Their progress was slow and very difficult, especially since the ground was soppy from the mixture of snow and several inches of mud. Their pace was also slowed by the need to avoid roads and move with caution so as not to be spotted by the rebels.

Despite their precautions, the De Grassis stumbled upon a party of rebels and narrowly escaped being captured. Blocking their path was a band of forty-two rebels patrolling the area, anxiously waiting for some sort of excitement to occur, perhaps even eager to take out their frustrations on loyalists. Thankfully, Charlotte's quick thinking saved them from being captured.

Taking matters into her own hands, she rode ahead of her father and sister to attract the rebel's attention, and was predictably stopped and questioned. With hearts pounding, not just for themselves but also for Charlotte, Philip and Cornelia moved like cats in the night so as not to be detected. They rode with painful slowness, afraid that their horses would snap a twig or suddenly whinny and give away their position. But the rebel's interrogation of Charlotte gave them the chance to quietly slip past without being heard or seen.

Though initially suspicious, the rebels didn't have any reason not to believe Charlotte's explanation for why she was out so late. Not deeming her a threat (what danger could a 10 year-old-girl pose?) they let her go and soon she had caught up to her father and her sister. Reunited, they continued on to Toronto.

When they arrived, they found the city in chaos and panic. There was a great deal of confusion about the size and location of the rebel army, and many people were convinced Toronto was about to fall. While at Parliament House, Cornelia volunteered to ride north along Yonge Street and gather information on behalf of the government. A stunned silence fell over the room as everyone in attendance suddenly looked at the young teen. Many chuckled to themselves, amused by her audacity and thinking "how could this child possibly help us?"

Philip De Grassi realized his daughter was serious and spoke up on her behalf, explaining that while his daughter was only thirteen years of age she was an excellent rider and had no fear. Bond Head saw some wisdom in her proposal, as well. Who would suspect a young girl of being a spy? She might succeed where a man could not. Reluctantly, he accepted Cornelia's offer.

A plan was formed. Cornelia would ride to Montgomery's Tavern on the pretence of wanting to know the price of a sleigh from a wheelwright whose shop was located beside the inn. She would only half listen to the wheelwright's answers, instead pay greater attention to the rebel army encamped nearby. This is just what she did, and the plan worked perfectly. While she had the wheelwright's attention and played the role of a potential customer, she took note of the number of rebels, their weapons and military training, as well as the fact that they were hungry and their morale was low.

After the wheelwright had answered her questions, she promised to return the next day with an answer as to whether her family wished to have a sleigh built. She politely said goodbye and mounted her horse. Just when she was about to breathe a sigh of relief, her mission done, a strong and firm hand grabbed hold of the horse's reins and ordered her to dismount. Cornelia looked down into the harsh face of a rebel. Suspicion was now in the air.

Feeling trapped and alone, Cornelia summoned all her courage in order to maintain her composure and cover story. She could not be afraid now, not when she had come so far and accomplished so much. But nothing she could say would convince the men to let her go. They were convinced she was a spy, and began to interrogate her in an effort to drag out the truth. After being questioned for what seemed like a lifetime, and just as she was beginning to fear she would be held prisoner indefinitely, Mackenzie arrived on the scene and proudly announced to the gathered rebels that a stage coach had been captured. This was a victory of sorts for men who thus far had only known defeat. They erupted with cheers as some headed for the stage coach to see the captured prize for themselves.

This was the opportunity that Cornelia was looking for. With the men suddenly distracted, she quickly hopped on her faithful horse and kicked it into a full gallop. Behind her, rebels shouted cries of alarm and muskets were raised. A thunder of bullets flew past her, with one hitting her saddle and another coming even closer to taking her life as it grazed her ear. Not daring to look back, she headed for Toronto.

Once there, she was taken before Sir Francis Bond Head and shared with the lieutenant-governor the intelligence she had gathered. With this information, the government realized they had extremely overestimated the size and strength of the rebel army, and as a result any thoughts of giving in to the rebels was abandoned and tossed aside. Feeling confident and realizing that the city was not going to fall to a massive rebel army, Bond Head decided to attack the rebels right away, before they grew stronger. This was a prudent decision, leading to victory at the Battle of Montgomery's Tavern and the quick and easy defeat of the rebellion.

By this stage, both Cornelia and Charlotte had already showed bravery multiple times, and yet they continued to demonstrate unusual fearlessness for their young age. Cornelia took pleasure in following the troops up Yonge Street, and watched the decisive battle as it unfolded at Montgomery's Tavern, perfectly composed despite the thundering of cannons and the roar of muskets. It was fitting that she should watch as the battle was won and Toronto saved, because had it not been for the intelligence she provided the panic-stricken government might have given up the city without a fight.

Charlotte, meanwhile, was having an adventure of her own. Despite being only ten years old, an officer begged her to carry vital information and correspondences because few horsemen were available. The young child took the challenge willingly, but once her task was completed she could not wait to get home and be with her mother once again. She was tired to the bone and emotionally drained. That evening, Charlotte decided her adventures were over and started the journey home.

Dangers lurked in the shadows, however, and the brave young soul was forced to confront her fears one more time. Darkness had settled upon the land like a heavy cloak as she rode toward the family farm. Without warning, she was caught in a rain of bullets from a large group of rebels who were guarding the road before her. Charlotte ducked reflexively and urged her horse to go faster, but she failed to dodge all of the bullets. She felt a sudden agonizing pain in her arm and could feel the warmth of blood running from within. Another bullet hit her horse, sending it into a panicked run. Charlotte desperately clung to the horse's mane as it jumped fences and crashed through bush, and though her arms and legs ached she managed to hold on long enough to calm her lathered mount and bring it under control. A while later, tired and in pain, the young girl succeeded in reaching her destination, her home.

With the loving arms of her mother once again holding

her, Charlotte could be a child once again. She could allow herself to feel fear, to cry from the agony of her wound. She was relieved and finally closed her eyes, allowing sleep to wash over her. But wait! What about Cornelia? Was she all right? Charlotte's eyes flew open, worried for her beloved sister. Suddenly a familiar smile appeared. Cornelia took her tiny hand in hers and whispered, "You're safe now." Sleep finally claimed Charlotte. The adventures of the De Grassi girls were over.

Elizabeth Lount

Elizabeth Lount stared up at Government House which, with its imposing height and cold grey stone walls, looked oppressive and cruel to the slight woman. A shiver of apprehension settled on her. She feared entering the building, but knew she must if she were to save the man she loved, the father of her children. She subconsciously smoothed the folds of her Sunday-best dress and fussed with her hair, realizing the importance of making a good impression on the lieutenant-governor, Sir George Arthur.

Taking a deep breath and tightly gripping a roll of paper, she mounted the steps on unsteady legs. Once inside, she was ushered into the presence of Arthur, a stiff and aloof-looking man who gazed at her coolly. There, she humbly introduced herself and presented the lieutenant-governor with a petition of clemency for her husband, Samuel Lount, one of the leaders of the ill-fated rebellion.[4] Elizabeth scanned the man's stern face, desperately searching for a flicker of compassion, a sign that he would commute the sentence of death by hanging. Would her valiant efforts be enough to save him?

Perhaps Elizabeth Lount also silently cursed her husband for bringing misfortune to the family. Just a few years prior, they had been living a peaceful and prosperous life, with hardly a concern in the world. In the past few months, thanks to Samuel's involvement in that debacle of a rebellion, their property had been seized, their name and reputation had been ruined, he was languishing in prison for treason, and she had faced death or injury on several occasions from individuals who hated what Samuel stood for. Their life, as they had previously known it, was over.

Elizabeth was born in 1793 in Oakland County, Michigan, to Daniel and Achsah Hollinshead.[5] In 1807 she married Samuel Lount and together they raised seven children in their Holland Landing home. At the time, Holland Landing was actually one of the most important communities north of Toronto and a major trading centre. Its mills served communities as far away as Innisfil in the north and Aurora in the south, and its wharfs comprised the major terminus for all shipping on Lake Simcoe. Samuel was one of the leading figures in the community; in addition to being a blacksmith, farmer, and surveyor, he was a politician in the Reform Party and a close associate of William Lyon Mackenzie.

Lount had a vested interest in bringing about change. He claimed to have evidence, which has never been substantiated, that showed that Sir Francis Bond Head had been giving land grants to settlers in exchange for their voting against Lount in the elections of 1836, an election that the popular Lount lost. In view of this real or imagined corruption, he became increasingly radicalized and came to the conclusion that change would only come about through a violent overthrow of the existing political system. Events came to a head in early winter of 1837, when Lount led an army of farmers down Yonge Street in support of Mackenzie's uprising.

When Samuel Lount made the decision to take up arms, did he bother to ask his wife her opinion on the matter? It's doubtful; in the early nineteenth century politics was not considered a subject for women. Did he even take into consideration the effect his decision would have upon her? In all likelihood he did not. Lount expected the rebellion would enjoy an easy and bloodless victory, and had no reason for concern regarding his wife's well-being.

As it turned out, the rebellion was quickly put down by government forces, and instead of returning home victorious Lount was forced to hide out in the woods as a fugitive, leaving Elizabeth and their young children at the mercy of vengeance-seeking loyalists who considered him a traitor. Twice in the days immediately following the Battle of Montgomery's Tavern, Elizabeth was confronted with mobs of angry men who threatened her life merely because she was married to one of the rebel ringleaders.

The first occurrence took place a mere day or two after the uprising was crushed. Moses Hayter, a family friend and the Barrie jailer, happened to be in Toronto collecting his ill son when the Rebellion of 1837 broke out.[6] Riding home, he stopped in Holland Landing to check on the well-being of the Lount family. He found Elizabeth cowering in fear, tears staining her cheeks, her hands shaking uncontrollably. In a voice croaked from crying, she explained that she had learned that a mob was on its way to burn the house and throw her and the children out into the cold. She was beside herself with fear.

Hayter gently held her hand and promised no harm would come to her. He then armed himself and awaited the vigilantes at the door. "Do you call yourselves Englishmen?" he challenged the mob of twenty or thirty men, each carrying a flaming torch. "I am an Englishman from the city of London, was an usher to the Duke of Wellington, where I was taught to know no fear in a just cause. I must sacredly declare that before you enter this house, with the intention of burning it down over the head of a defenceless woman and her children, you will have to walk over the dead body of an Englishman, but not before I will take good account of at least one of you!"

A murmur went through the mob. They hadn't expected resistance, and their courage began to fail them. Hayter changed tactics at this point: "If you only knew the character of the man whom you are seeking for his life as well as I do, you would retire in shame," he said. "Once he saved me and my family from starvation when that fate stared us in the face. And hundreds can testify that he has reached out a helping hand to those who were in great need."

At this point, the mob hesitated as if unsure what to do. Whether moved by his speech, or simply afraid of facing an armed man instead of a helpless woman, the vigilantes seemed to lose their lust for vengeance. Slowly, in singles and pairs, they turned for home. Elizabeth Lount was safe for the moment, thanks to the brave stand made by Moses Hayter.

A few days later, however, she once again found herself in peril. This time Stephen Howard, a neighbour, received word that another armed mob was working its way up Yonge Street to burn Lount's home and arrest his family.[7] Howard raced to warn Elizabeth so that she might escape with some of her valuables. He also sent his son, Stephen, then all of thirteen years of age, with a team of oxen and a sleigh to assist her. Once the sleigh was loaded with as many possessions as possible, young Howard headed off for an isolated barn that would be the refuge of Elizabeth and her children until matters settled down. Unfortunately, they hadn't gone very far before they were overtaken by hell-bent loyalist riders and compelled to drive to McLeod's Tavern, in Aurora. There they were held captive.

When Stephen Howard learned of their capture, he raced to secure his son's release. After much negotiation, the captives were set free but their possessions confiscated. Elizabeth never did receive the bulk of her belongings, and when the Howard oxen were finally returned weeks later they were in such bad shape as to be all but worthless as draft animals.

Things continued to go from bad to worse for Elizabeth Lount. Shortly afterwards, she learned that her husband had been captured as he tried to flee across Lake Erie in a rowboat. She watched with growing despair as Samuel and another rebel leader, Peter Matthews, were charged with high treason. And her heart sank when she heard that Chief Justice Sir John Beverley Robinson, who presided over the trials, believed that "some examples should be made in the way of capital punishment," and had therefore sentenced Samuel Lount and Peter Matthews to be hung.

Rather than wallow in misery, Elizabeth found the strength to fight for her husband's life. She began a petition for clemency and got eight thousand people to sign it, including many loyalists who believed the sentence too harsh. Her passion and determination moved many men, but the question remained: would it move Sir George Arthur, the Lieutenant-Governor of Upper Canada and the only man who could reduce the sentences?

When Elizabeth Lount presented the petition and pleaded her husband's case, Arthur remained unmoved.

He had formerly been the governor of the prison colony of Van Dieman's Land, where he had presided over anguish, misery and despair and had grown accustomed to administering harsh justice with the chain, the lash, and the rope. Compassion was foreign to his nature and he easily held his emotions in check. Arthur refused to commute the sentence. Elizabeth, who up until now had demonstrated remarkable poise and strength, went to pieces. She fell to her knees and begged him not to hang her husband and leave her children fatherless. She wept and pleaded, but Arthur would not listen to reason.

The government was determined to use Lount and Matthews as examples of the price of rebellion. They were led to the gallows on the morning of April 12, 1838. When the trap door opened and Samuel plunged to his death, a part of Elizabeth died as well. She was inconsolable, and fled Canada for the United States where she died years later in 1878, still mourning the loss of her husband and still scarred by her experiences during the rebellion of 1837.

Notes

Chapter 3: Colonels Moodie and Bridgford

1. For Captain Hugh Stewart's account of Colonel Moodie's death, see Read and Stagg, *The Rebellion of 1837 in Upper Canada*, 144–45.

2. Biographical information on Colonel Robert Moodie comes from the files of the Richmond Hill Public Library, as well as from Stamp, *Early Days in Richmond Hill*.

3. The history of the New Brunswick Fencibles is detailed in Chartrand, *British Forces in North America 1793–1815*.

4. From Capt. Stewart's account in Read and Stagg.

5. Ibid.

6. Many of the details on Captain Robert Bridgford come courtesy of Dinah Cruse-Hunter, a descendant, a living history re-enacter and member of the Incorporated Militia of Upper Canada, and an authority on Bridgford. A detailed outline of Bridgford's life, as written by Cruse-Hunter, is available online at www.imuc.org/bridgeford.pdf.

Chapter 4: Hotels in the Rebellion

1. Guillet, *Pioneer Days*, 144.

2. Information on Thomas Gamble comes from the files of the Elman C. Campbell Museum, in Newmarket, Ontario.

3. More extensive details on the community of Armitage can

be found in Gillham, *Early Settlements of King Township,*
5–11.

4. Much of the information on Joseph Milbourne comes from
the files of the Thornhill Archives.

5. The Queen's Hotel was a haven for Reformers and their
sympathizers. David Gibson, a leading member of the
movement, gave numerous fiery speeches there and, as his
diary notes, "on June 27, 1836, I went to Milburn's Inn on
Yonge Street and appeared as the candidate for the riding
and had a majority the first day."

6. The Queen's Hotel thrived until 1869 when, on February
12, a fire broke out. Though the Thornhill Fire Company
and volunteers managed to save much of the contents the
building itself was burned to the ground. A new Queen's
Hotel was raised on the site and lasted until it too was
burned to the ground in 1906. It was replaced by a stone
residence.

Chapter 5: Chief Yellowhead and Natives

1. Much of the information on Chief Yellowhead comes
from C. H. Hale's article in Ireton et al., *Orillia Portraits,*
23–26. Also see the entry in the Dictionary of Canadian
Biography online at www.biographi.ca/009004-119.01-e.
php?BioId=38742.

2. The Battle of York (as Toronto was then known) took place
on April 27, 1813. An American amphibious assault succeeded in driving out the small British garrison and seizing

a large quantity of supplies. The Americans occupied York for a week and then re-embarked on their ships and left.

3. The Ojibwa experience at Orillia is covered in greater depth in Randy Richmond's *The Orillia Spirit.*

4. A concise by detailed account of the Indians during the War of 1812 can be found in *The War of 1812*, by Carl Benn.

5. An account of minorities during the 1837 Rebellion, including the role of African-Canadians, can be found in Duncan and Lockwood, *1837 Rebellion Remembered.*

Chapter 6: Outlaws and Villains

1. Arculus, *Mayhem to Murder*, provides a detailed account of the Markham Gang, including much information on Henry Johnson and other prominent members.

2. Ibid., 61.

3. The *British Colonist*, Tuesday, November 3, 1846.

4. The *Brockville Recorder*, November 12, 1846.

5. Accounts of Johnson's life in Stouffville come from files of the Whitchurch-Stouffville Museum.

Chapter 7: The Sharon Martyrs

1. Much of the biographical information on James Kavanagh comes courtesy of the Sharon Temple, which over the years has done extensive genealogical studies of the various members of the Children of Peace. See http://www.sharontemple.ca/index.php?option=com_content&view=article&id=9&Itemid=17

2. The history of the 99th Foot during its time in British North

America is detailed in Chartrand's *British Forces.*

3. Files from the Sharon Temple.

4. Files from the Sharon Temple. It should be noted that Kavanagh lingered for several days before dying in a hospital on December 12. His wife, Elizabeth, never remarried. She eventually joined her daughter and son-in-law in New York State, where she died in 1875.

5. As with Kavanagh, much of the biographical information for James Henderson comes courtesy of the Sharon Temple.

6. Extensive information on the Hughes family can be found at http://www.sharontemple.ca/pdf/Genealogy%20%28By%20Family%29/family_hughes.pdf

7. The *Patriot and Farmer's Monitor,* December 8, 1837. The paper describes the brief skirmish: "Two small parties, under Mr. Sheriff Jarvis and Mr. Cameron, advanced last night a short distance up Yonge Street, and had some skirmishing with the Rebels, of whom one was killed and two others wounded; the rest, number not known, taking to their heels with a most hearty good-will."

Chapter 8: Women and Children

1. More details on the De Grassi girls than could be fitted within the confines of this entry, and information on why the girls' heroism was forgotten, can be found in two excellent sources: Charles Sauriol's *Remembering the Don,* 129–34, and W. Stewart Wallace's article published by the Royal

Society of Canada, "The Story of Charlotte and Cornelia de Grassi."

2. Information on Philip De Grassi's life can be found in Wallace, *The Macmillan Dictionary of Canadian Biography.*

3. As quoted from De Grassi's diary in *Remembering the Don.*

4. Details on Samuel Lount can be found online at www.sharontemple.ca/pdf/Biographies/bio_samuel_Lount.pdf.

5. Extensive genealogical information on Elizabeth Lount's family can be found online at www.anthonyhollingshead.org/mike4.htm.

6. Moses Hayter moved to London in 1832 and settled in Innisfil near Big Bay Point. His friendship with Lount was forged when the latter provided food aid that prevented the starvation of Hayter and his family during the first harsh winter in the new country. Hayter moved to Barrie in 1843 when he was appointed the Simcoe District's first jailer. He resigned in 1855 when his wife was assaulted by an escaping prisoner, after which he farmed and operated a sawmill. He died in 1865.

7. Stephen Howard operated a tavern in Aurora that was used by participants on both sides of the rebellion, but otherwise played no role in the unfolding events.

Bibliography

Arculus, Paul. *Mayhem to Murder: The History of the Markham Gang.*
Port Perry, ON: Observer Publishing, 1993.

Berchem, F. R. The *Yonge Street Story 1793–1860: An Account from
Letters, Diaries and Newspapers.* Toronto: Natural Heritage/Natural
History Inc., 1996.

Benn, Carl. *The War of 1812.* Essential Histories. New York: Routledge,
2003.

Brown, Sheila Jean, ed. *Researching Yonge Street.* Toronto: Ontario
Genealogical Society, Toronto Branch, 1996.

Chartrand, René. *British Forces in North America 1793–1815.* Oxford:
Osprey, 1998.

Cruse-Hunter, Dinah. "The Colonel: The Life & Times of Col. David
Bridgford, 1791–1860," Military Re-Enactment Society of Canada,
http://www.imuc.org/bridgeford.pdf.

Duncan, Dorothy, and Glenn J. Lockwood. "Introduction." *1837
Rebellion Remembered: Papers Presented at the 1837 Rebellion
Remembered Conference...* Willowdale: Ontario Historical Society,
1988.

Gibson, David. Personal Diary. Notes obtained courtesy of staff at
Gibson House Museum, Toronto, Ontario.

Gillham, Elizabeth McClure. *Early Settlements of King Township,
Ontario.* King City: Municipality of the Township of King, 1984.

Guillet, E. C. *Pioneer Days in Upper Canada.* Toronto: University of
Toronto Press, 1965.

Ireton, Nora, Ruth Thompson and Grace Crooks, eds. *Orillia Portraits*,
2nd ed., revised. Orillia: Orillia Historical Society, 1966.

Read, Colin, and Ronald J. Stagg. *The Rebellion of 1837 in Upper
Canada.* Ottawa: Carleton University Press, 1985.

Richmond, Randy. *The Orillia Spirit: An Illustrated History of Orillia*. Toronto: Dundurn Press, 1996.

Stamp, Robert M. *Early Days in Richmond Hill: A History of the Community to 1930*. Richmond Hill: Richmond Hill Public Library Board, 1991.

Sauriol, Charles. *Remembering the Don: A Rare Record of Earlier Times within the Don River Valley*. Scarborough, ON: Consolidated Amethyst Communications, 1981.

Wallace, W. Stewart, ed. *The Macmillan Dictionary of Canadian Biography*, 3rd ed. London: Macmillan, 1963.

———. "The Story of Charlotte and Cornelia de Grassi." *Proceedings and Transactions of the Royal Society of Canada*, 3rd ser., 35, no. 2 (May, 1941):147–51.

Photo Credits

Courtesy of Georgina Pioneer Museum, photographer Philip Rose Donohue: 24; Courtesy of Toronto Public Library: cover, 40, 92; Author's Collection: 53; Courtesy Niagara Falls Public Library: 84

Acknowledgements

The authors wish to acknowledge the following individuals and organizations for providing assistance in writing this book: Cam Knight and the staff at the Richmond Hill Public Library, who tracked down historic images on our behalf; the Royal Society of Canada; Kathleen Fry at the King Township Museum and Beth Sinyard of the Elman C. Campbell Museum in Newmarket. Finally, we extend our appreciation and respect to members of local historical societies who endeavour to preserve the past, often without the credit they deserve. Writing this book would have been a lot more difficult and time-consuming had it not been for their work.

We would also like to thank Nancy Sewell of James Lorimer and Company for supporting this project and giving us her valued assistance and understanding during the lengthy process of writing it.

Andrew Hind adds: I would like to thank Maria da Silva for her ability to bring characters to life, to allow the reader to feel a connection with people long dead. History, after all, is more than a collection of facts and dates—history is about people and the emotions that shape their lives.

About the Authors

Andrew Hind is a freelance writer who lives in Bradford, Ontario. His feature articles have appeared in magazines and newspapers across Canada, in the United States and in Britain. Andrew developed a passion for history early on, especially for unusual and obscure events and people that are typically overlooked or quickly forgotten. He hopes, through his writing, to bring these fascinating stories to light for a modern audience.

Maria da Silva is also a resident of Bradford. She frequently contributes articles to local publications such as *Footprints*, *Simcoe Sideroads*, *Muskoka Magazine*, and the *Muskoka Sun*. Maria is originally from Portugal, a country rich in history, but she never dreamed that her future would lead her into writing about the past.

Andrew and Maria have co-authored six books, including *Strange Events of Ontario* and *Ghost Town Stories of Ontario*, both published by James Lorimer and Company.

Index

Index